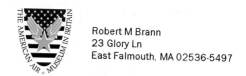
Wings Over Istanbul

D1597459

Russell Boardman and John Polando aboard the Cape Cod *in Istanbul, Turkey.*

Wings Over Istanbul

THE LIFE AND FLIGHTS OF A PIONEER AVIATOR

Johnnie Polando

PETER E. RANDALL PUBLISHER
PORTSMOUTH, NH
2000

I lovingly dedicate this book to John's children John, Jr., JoAnne, James, and David

I am deeply indebted to the Massachusetts Aviation Historical Society, and most specifically, Stuart Downing and William Deane for their countless hours of work in editing and, in many cases, verifying the specific information regarding types of aircraft and locations. I thank our son James for his very important part in preparing the material for publication.

And to the wonderful friends who made John's life so special.

Dorothy Polando

Copyright © 2000 by Dorothy Polando
Printed in the United States of America
Design: Tom Allen, Pear Graphics Design

Peter E. Randall Publisher
Box 4726
Portsmouth, NH 03802-4726

Distributed by University Press of New England: Hanover and London

Library of Congress Cataloging-in-Publication data
Polando, Johnnie, 1901-1985.
    Wings over Istanbul : the life and flights of a pioneer aviator / Johnnie Polando.
    p. cm.
    ISBN 0-914339-84-2 (alk. paper)
    1. Polando, Johnnie, 1901-1985. 2. Air pilots—United States—
        Biography. I. Title.
TL540.P587 A3 2000
629.13'092—dc21
[B]
                                                                00-024619

Contents

1

Where It All Began

To say that I was born to fly would be presuming a lot, and the Lord knows I have presumed enough without making any such claim. To say that I am never content to wait for things to happen, that I am always early and I am always ready; to say that each day, each hour is a challenge, to say that I am restless, curious, eager and willing would be more to the point. To say that I am more at home in the air than on the ground would be even more accurate. I was a good automobile mechanic but I excelled in airplane mechanics and loved the challenge. For each new problem opened up such possibilities for solutions and improvement that I could hardly wait to begin. My mechanics license AP 1330 and my pilot's license No. 5614 are things of which I am very proud. But, this is getting way ahead of my story. For you to make any sense out of this we should start at the beginning.

I was born on September 6, 1901, into an Italian family with all the ritual and discipline of the old-time Italians. My family knew no different.

Papa's name was George B. (the B chosen at random when the immigration insisted on a middle initial) Polando. Papa was the son of a seaman and was born about 1850. He did not remember his mother and when he was twelve years old his father was missing at sea and presumed dead. George's father had placed him with a family in Genoa while at sea, and there he remained after his father was lost.

The dream of many of the young men of Italy was to come to American and George was no different. When he was in his late teens he married the oldest daughter of his benefactor and he provided passage for his daughter and her new husband to emigrate. Their most immediate need when they arrived was to find shelter and food. George used some of what little they had to purchase peaches and sell them on street corners. He was a tall, slender winsome young man with a ready wit and charm. He worked diligently at his chosen trade and before long the crate on the corner became a pushcart and then one, then two, and finally three fine fruit and tobacco stores in Lynn where the young couple had come to live.

Within a few years George and his wife had four children. With several children, a handsome home and a thriving fruit business, they hired a girl to care for the children in the lovely big house on Rogers Avenue.

Mary Louise Arata, the daughter of an Italian-English tutor, who worked with Harvard students on languages, was hired. She and her sisters had been raised in East Boston, were members of the Catholic church, where Mary sang masses and, in general, had a happy childhood. She and Sophie were very close and remained so during their lifetimes.

Mary was possibly fourteen when she came to Rogers Avenue and George was in his mid-thirties. Mrs. Polando died very young when George was only thirty-nine. After a suitable time George asked Mr. Arata for Mary's hand in marriage. She was under eighteen but permission was granted and they were wed in 1889.

Whether in deference to Mary, which I doubt, or just the need for a bigger house in which to raise the children, George purchased a large piece of land on Forest Hill Avenue at the lower edge of Lovers' Leap, abutting the Pine Grove cemetery. After the sale of the house on Rogers Avenue, they rented a cottage on Maple Street while their new home was being built. It was in this house that Mary and George's first child, Violet, was born in 1890.

The big house on Forest Hill Avenue was finally completed and ready to welcome the family. It was a great Victorian mansion with a veranda across the front reached by wide, inviting front steps. The door opened into a spacious front hall with black and white parquet floor and an elegant staircase with a handsome newelpost and graced with a huge Boston fern. The first floor was comprised of a parlor (open only on formal occasions), the library, the great dining room, the fragrant kitchen and the pantry. The kitchen boasted the newest woodstove of iron with nickel trim, a soapstone sink and an oak ice chest. Upstairs were four bedrooms and a bath. The only central heat was in the library, where we spent much of our time, and in the dining room and the bathroom upstairs. Pa and Ma had the front bedroom, and eventually they would fill the other three bedrooms with us children.

Mary was only three or four years older than Pa's oldest child. Whether these children had left home or were moved to Forest Hill Avenue I can't remember. I don't recall seeing much of them.

Each of us children arrived at about three year intervals. Little George was born about 1893, Francis in 1896, and Harry in 1899. I was born in 1901, Leo in 1904 and Alberta in 1907. Harry died in infancy. Aside from scrapes, bruises, childhood illnesses and, probably thanks to the smelly bags of herbs we wore under our clothing in winter to ward off sickness, we were fine.

No house in those days was complete without a pantry. I remember it fondly, with its cookie crock always full of goodies and the leftovers that we were allowed to snack on left there covered with inverted soup plates. I can still recall the marvelous smells that originated in that kitchen. I remember too the hot bricks that were gingerly taken off the stove at bedtime and wrapped in flannel to warm our feet in those cold beds upstairs. Violet shared a room with Alberta, George and Francis shared, and Leo had to put up with me as a roommate.

In addition to being a wife, mother, housekeeper, cook and laundress Mary was a clerk and bookkeeper at the store. She was good at that too. She joked with the customers and was a whiz with figures. You probably remember when a clerk would take a brown paper bag and mark down the price of each item as the customer got his groceries. Well, Ma could add that column faster than any clerk Pa ever had, according to him. She was such an asset to the business that shortly after each of us children was born she would find someone to care for us and return to the store to work with Pa.

The demands of an active fruit and tobacco business were many. Each morning found Pa driving his team and wagon along the bumpy, dusty Lynn-Revere road before the pale light of dawn found its way from the sea to the marsh and beyond. The Boston open market was a noisy scramble by the time the retail merchants drove their empty rigs over the rough paving stones at Quincy Market and Faneuil Hall to begin their daily haggle for produce. As we grew up, Pa had each of us accompany him occasionally to market in summer. It was exciting at first, but it didn't take us long to decide that this was not the life for us. The hours were too long and we all had other interests.

I can see Pa now sitting proudly in our Sunday carriage with his team of handsome horses. He carried himself with dignity, and rightly so, for he had come a long way in life. On the Sabbath he wore his derby, a necktie, his well-tailored suit and his white celluloid collar; weekdays it was a straw hat, a striped shirt, a bowtie, his butchers apron and the white celluloid collar. He was taller and slimmer than any of his sons and ramrod straight but there was a glint of humor and a bit of a roving eye when Ma wasn't in view.

She, on the other hand, was tiny, had a sharp tongue and kept a close rein on Pa. I think she was really the boss, and I know for a fact that she kept a watchful eye on the till, far more than Pa. When they worked late at the store, it was she who arranged a basket to carry home with fruit on top of the bundles of cash. The walk from Monroe Street and Central Avenue to Forest Hill Avenue and Polando Terrace was more than a mile. Life at home didn't suffer from the long hours at the store. On Christmas Eve she would go to work in the kitchen after midnight Mass and often cook all night so that our dinner on Christmas Day included all the holiday delicacies to which we were accustomed.

Of all the kids, I was closest in age and in affection to Leo, my younger brother. He had to be the kindest, most trusting, most willing person I have ever known. He had complete, and often misplaced, faith in me and I used him. I recall when my friend Eldred and I went duck hunting on the marsh. We were all of fourteen at the time and Leo tagged along to be with the "big kids." Well, one of us downed a duck, which dropped into the freezing cold water of the river. Having no dog to retrieve it we, half-jokingly, told Leo to go and get it. He did. He nearly froze and almost drowned in the river, but he got the duck and brought it back. I don't think either of us really expected him to do our bidding but we should have guessed. By the time we got Leo home his clothes had begun to stiffen with the cold. We were soundly thrashed and rightly so.

As with all families, there were chores to do. With the Polandos chores meant putting in time at the store, a job we rapidly grew to hate. In addition to sweeping floors, there were strawberries to be picked over and repacked in little wooden baskets. A skillful fruit dealer could make fourteen pints out of ten with careful handling and father was a skillful merchant.

The tiresome job of roasting the peanuts in the gas fired, glass-sided pushcart was another chore that fell to us boys. It was necessary to crank the machine constantly by hand to keep the nuts tossing so they would not burn. "Polando's Peanuts Can't Be Beat" was our slogan. I can still smell the fragrance of roasting nuts as they danced crazily in the pushcart. The aroma drifted tantalizingly all the way down Central Square to the depot where the narrow gauge railway disgorged its weary Boston travelers. For a nickel they could fill their pockets with warm peanuts. Many a traveler made a nightly stop for the tempting morsels and a cheery "Hello" from Pa. As for us boys, tired of the constant cranking, we discovered that, with a little practice, a strong arm and fast legs, we could crank up the machine to a pitch where it would run just long enough on its own to permit us to dash to the candy counter and grab a handful of peppermints and return before the peanuts burned. Any miscalculations, however, would bring the wrath of the devil on us and a well-aimed boot to the britches. I must admit I got my share.

I made lots of good friends as I was growing up and some of them are still around to reminisce with. My closest friend in my teen years was Eldred Rhodes, my partner in the duck hunting caper. If there was mischief to be found, we found it. Fourth of July prompted the stealing of privies for bonfires. I still chuckle when I think of the surprised and angry neighbors running out for their first visit of the day in slippers and robe staring in disbelief at the gaping hole left uncovered by our theft. One of our other pranks was to pour gasoline in the trolley tracks and set it afire. It makes a trail of smoke and fire that is exciting on a dark night. Eldred and I help set up tents when the circus came to town in exchange for passes to the show. Famished from all that hard work, we stole bottles of milk off the nearby stoops to fill our empty bellies.

I was a great one for bringing home stray puppies. We had a mud room off the kitchen and I can remember slipping a puppy under a bushel basket to keep it out of sight. The little fellow cried and yipped so loudly that it was only a short time before everyone in the house knew where it was and what I had done. I was permitted to keep this dog and he was my constant companion for a long time. In fact, I have never been without a dog for any length of time except when I was in the service.

Now, if you were looking for me in a crowd when I was young, you would look for the skinniest, brown haired, brown eyed, dark skinned, runny nosed kid in the neighborhood. I was the quickest too, I ran, jumped, and dodged faster than any of the kids because

I managed to get into the most trouble, and not always of my own making, and screwed up more times than anyone else I knew. Ma and I had a kind of game we played. I'd dash into the kitchen ducking as Ma would swing on me. "What'd I do?" I'd shout. "You musta done something" she'd reply as I scrambled out of reach.

I spent a lot of time climbing the coal pile to get out of Pa's grasp when he charged down the cellar steps with the whipping stick because I had gotten into trouble again. I couldn't resist throwing snowballs at the ragman, catching snakes and toads that ended up in school desks, or crawling up the circular fire slide at the schoolhouse. I was the distraction of all the teachers. The singing teacher hated me because I deliberately sang off key, The principal hated me even more because I dodged the blow with the rubber hose that was aimed at me and it hit his gouty knee. I can't say how many times I was expelled. I wasn't taught what I really wanted to know. The business about the Civil War and George Washington at Valley Forge left me cold. I liked to read but I didn't do very well. I learned my sums but the other stuff seemed dumb. I just couldn't concentrate on things that didn't work such as engines or involve action like baseball. Baseball is, and always has been, one of my passions. Anyone sending me to the store on an errand was not likely to get what I was sent for promptly, if at all, if I found something better to do.

As for school, I finally quit in the fifth grade, a minor matter I omitted on my air force enlistment form. I thought I had all the education I would ever need and more than I could stomach of the routine. How wrong I was and how I have lived to regret it.

Pa was furious with me for quitting school. Ma was even madder but they had done just about everything they could to make me go to school. I had finally worn them down. Since I was no longer in school Pa said that I would have to go to work. I got a job scraping the hair off hides at Agoos Leather Company. Even that stinking job was better than school and I worked there for some time.

My next job was repairing shoe machines for stitching vamps on shoes. That was all right until someone accused me of ogling the girl's legs when I was repairing the foot treadles so I was fired. Actually I wasn't eyeing the girls. Girls didn't interest me that much at the time.

Then I worked for a company that made chopping blocks for

butcher shops. These two jobs were brought home to me recently when I got an old factory sewing machine from my son, David. He didn't even know that I had worked in the factory. Shortly thereafter my son Jim bought an old, used, swayback chopping block for his kitchen that had been made about the time I worked in their factory. It has four mismatched legs. Because I am a "casual carpenter" at best it has been assumed that I had built that particular block. Perhaps I did.

When my friend Eldred and I were in our teens we were hired to drive funeral cars for Eldred's father, T.W.Rhodes. It was 1918 in the dark days of the influenza epidemic. All the funeral homes were working long hours trying to keep abreast of the flood of victims of the dread disease. Old enough to drive but too young to be impressed by the solemnity of the situation, we made bets on who could drive the mourners back to the funeral home the fastest. I don't recall who won but it most certainly was not the bereaved. They were terrified, and with good cause. I am certainly glad my kids were not like me.

We had some wonderful times in our big house on the side of the hill. Pa had a garden, terraced because of the slope and probably because that is the way he remembered the gardens in Genoa, his old home. The hill was so steep that the water ran in great rivulets down toward our house and Pa had to dig holes through the foundation and trench the floor of the basement to permit the water to run through freely.

On Sundays at our house, mother's long table was surrounded by neighbors, family and friends. I can't remember many Sundays after Mass when we had no company. Ma set a marvelous table. The mountainous portions of ravioli or polenta were accompanied by platters of meat, vegetables, homemade breads, salads, and wine—gallons of father's fine wine made in our cellar. Because he was in the fruit business the kegs in the basement were brimming with the most delicious wines made from choice grapes with great care. Many of our guests departed bearing gifts from his famous kegs. As I recall, many of our guests were often so full of fine food and wine that their steps were uncertain as they descended the long flight of stairs from our piazza as they headed for home.

Each of us kids succeeded in his or her own way. George was a commercial artist and commissioned to paint a huge sign on the side of one of the buildings in Lynn, standing on a scaffolding when he was still in kneepants. Violet was an aspiring pianist. Francis, using the name of Frank Walker, became a minor league baseball player until he was injured sliding into second base. He then established a successful sign painting business in Florida. Pa took Violet and young George to Genoa when Violet was eighteen to show them off and visit old friends. His quest was unsuccessful for no one remembered him or the family with whom he had lived. Alberta and I didn't have much in common. She went to business school and got an excellent office job. Leo was my favorite. He was the most loving and kindest member of the whole family.

One of the first things that my artist brother, George, painted was the bob-sled that he and brother Francis built. They called it the "Scream." It went like the wind and all the kids could be heard shrieking as they flew down the steep hill of Lover's Leap. Forest Hill Avenue is so steep that it was rarely used by anyone aside from panting pedestrians but it descended into North Franklin and was a long and reasonably safe place to coast.

2
My First Encounter

·

In about 1918, I got a job as a driver for C. E. Whitten, the Buick Dealer in Lynn. Automobiles built in Flint, Michigan, were not shipped by freight cars at that time so drivers were hired to bring them east. I was young and green. I'd never been farther than Boston or North Grafton so this was a great adventure to me. As it turned out, it was also an education.

A group of us recruited to drive the cars east were given train tickets and berths for the overnight trip west. The men I went with were considerably older than I, so I was the butt of their jokes. First they told me that the little hammock in the berth was to keep me from falling into the aisle on the curves. I was instructed to hang on to it securely at all times. One of the curves, the Sandwich Curve they called it, was supposedly so sharp that the engineer could shake hands with the man in the observation car. It took only one trip to nullify their claims but they enjoyed the joshing and so did I. The difference in our ages did cause one problem. Once they were through driving for the day they would head for the nearest bar-room. I tailed after them only once and was promptly and uncere-moniously thrown out and had to wait for them on the sidewalk.

I was still with Whitten in 1919 but had graduated from driving cars to repairing them. I liked mechanics and was doing well in that field. One day, though, a very special day as it turned out, I jeopar-dized my job and found a new friend.

On this particular day in 1920 a doctor's car had been outfitted with new brake bands. I was assigned to test them on the old dirt road, now the Lynnway, which was the usual test course.

As I drove down the rutted road that warm, sunny day I was startled to see an airplane on the grassy strip near the shore. Its lines were far different from the sleek contours of modern aircraft but the fascination was there. This was my first intimate contact with a real airplane. There it was, shining in the morning sun. It was wood, metal, linen, and wire and was, without a doubt, the most beautiful and exciting thing I had ever seen.

In a flash I forgot the doctor's car and was striding across the grass toward the plane and its pilot. I don't remember what we said to each other but I am sure he was floored with the flood of questions from this greenhorn. I learned that he was Lieutenant Thomas F. Havey and I guess I told him my name but it was of little consequence at that particular time. My admiration and enthusiasm were evident. I circled the Canadian Jenny taking in everything he was telling me about the operation of the plane. The time flew by and, because he was unable to leave the plane, I volunteered to get him a bottle of milk and a sandwich. My reward was permission to sit in the cockpit, caress the smooth fabric of her fuselage, and wings—in short to make love to my new mistress.

Ecstasy distorts one's priorities. When I finally returned the doctor's car to Whitten's at five o'clock I was fired on the spot. I must admit that this was not the first time I had been unduly detained on the job for Whitten but never had I been gone so long.

Now, forcibly retired, I spent all my time at the Lynnway with my new friend but my "affair" with his beautiful ship and my friendship with this remarkable man were destined to be all too brief.

The lieutenant had been hired to fly a parachutist by the name of Henry Smith to Salisbury Beach where he was scheduled to jump to attract a crowd to the famous spot. The stowage of the parachute was under the fuselage of the aircraft where it was secured by heavy straps. The weight of the jumper would release the straps then the jumper would pull the release ring on his harness and shake the heavy canvas chute vigorously to make it open. The parachute was packed tightly with layers of newspaper tucked into the folds so that the fabric would not stick to itself.

All was in readiness. Lieutenant Havey and Smith climbed aboard then taxied to the end of the grassy area, revved up the engine, roared down the strip. Havey pulled back on the joystick lifting the plane gently into the wind. It had hardly left the ground when the wind, somehow, caught a corner of the folded parachute, whipped it open and flung it around the tail section of the aircraft. The plane crashed in the middle of the old dirt road. It was hard to believe that there were two bodies buried in the pile of debris that had been a JN4 Jenny. I was not the only spectator and all of us scrambled to tear away the rubble and free the two men. We worked feverishly but in vain for both had presumably died on impact. These were my friends who had laughed and talked with me only minutes ago. I was crushed. Unfortunately, this was only the first of many mishaps involving airplanes, my good friends and me.

I guess I am a diehard. Flying is a disease. It enters the bloodstream and, perhaps like malaria, is incurable. At times it is dormant but never dead. Even the untimely deaths on the Lynnway could not discourage me. I became more determined than ever to be a part of this fascinating if often dangerous vocation.

Later in 1920, when I was working at Daley's Garage a new mode of flying captured my imagination. I met Professor Harold Kates from Newburyport, an intrepid flyer who was a hot air balloonist. What a challenge, flight without power. Something new and mysterious had been added to my ever expanding horizon.

The good professor was operating on a hand-to-mouth basis. His office, hotel, and shop were the backseat of his old car. As luck would have it, he needed a "fireman." I was just his man.

The process of inflating the huge balloon was complex. It required at least two men to set the apparatus in place. Several additional men were needed to handle the restraining lines as the bag filled, so eager spectators were pressed into service.

First the frame was erected and the canvas balloon was hauled into place on the framework with a block and tackle. Then a trench was dug in the earth to contain a bonfire. An empty open-ended oil drum with a screen on the top was placed over the trench and the hot air would rise through it into the balloon. The fire was then built and stoked with kindling quickly so that the hot air would fill the bag rapidly. The fireman then checked inside the balloon choking and using the fire extinguisher to kill live sparks. This process continued until the balloon lifted gently off the frame. With each burst of hot air the heavy balloon tugged more urgently at the mooring lines until it was light enough to fly free. Just before the lines were dropped, a large splash of kerosene was thrown on the fire for the all-important last surge of hot air before lift-off.

On the day most vivid in my memory, I had stoked and extinguished with my usual zeal. The big bag was moving restlessly and the people on the mooring lines were impatiently waiting the words "let go." The time had come for that dash of kerosene but, suddenly, the funnel tipped, the splash of kerosene missed its mark and, in the excitement, the lines were released. The spectators and I watched in awe. The great bag moved slowly just above the trees and houses for a block or so then bumped on the slate roof of the Methodist church. Thoroughly disgusted and a bit scared, the professor climbed clumsily out of the basket and on to the roof as the balloon swung away. Sad to relate, the roof was equipped with the metal spikes designed to break up snow and ice as it melts and, although the spikes prevented the professor from falling from the slippery slate roof, they managed to remove a great deal of skin and they damaged, almost beyond repair, his reputation as an expert balloonist. The balloon fared only a little better. It drifted into Euclid Avenue near Delansky's Florist shop before draping itself, languidly across the streetcar trolley lines shorting out the power and obstructing traffic. It caused great confusion on the busy avenue. Needless to say, blameless as I thought I was, this job too terminated.

3

The Saugus Race Track

By late 1920 I was a regular at the Saugus Race track, which was used as an airstrip after its original purpose was abandoned. Prior to 1910 it had been one of the most elegant horse tracks in New England. So well patronized was the track that a fifty-room hotel was built to accommodate the guests. On July 11, 1911 Harry Atwood, who now used the track as a flying field, put Saugus in the annals of aviation history by setting a long-distance record flying from Saugus to Washington, D.C. The track then became known as Atwood Park and Harry taught flying to the venturesome.

Another wonderful pilot and fine man used this same strip for student pilots. He was H. Roy Waite, a student of the Wright brothers. He was teaching flying as early as 1912. When the Smithsonian Institution was assembling the Wright brothers plane for the museum, it was Roy Waite who assisted in rebuilding the fragile craft used at Kitty Hawk in December 1903 when, for the first time, the flight of man in heavier than air craft was no longer an impractical dream. Roy, who died only a few years ago, saw seventy-five years of progress in the field of aviation. Men of his caliber, pioneers in every sense of the word, have contributed tremendously to our way of life. Many, like Roy, have done it quietly, unobtrusively, finding joy and satisfaction in accomplishment and not expecting or receiving any special recognition.

In 1920 Al Valliere, a remarkably capable mechanic and innovator, was operating in one of the old buildings on the track. I was working with and for him as a part-time mechanic. We were using one side of the old track as a landing strip.

Al and I had little money, just the burning desire to make planes fly. We were destined to lose every one of the three by accident. The third plane was the Avro that Reverend Belvin Maynard flew in Rutland, Vermont, but more of that later.

TAKE A FLIGHT
IN AN AEROPLANE
At CLIFTONDALE AVIATION FIELD, Cliftondale, Mass.
With H. ROY WAITE

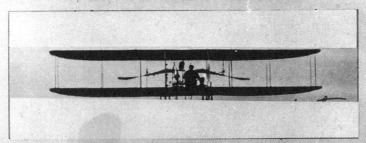

In His BURGESS-WRIGHT BIPLANE. Safest Aeroplane Known to Date.

Passengers
Carried

Everybody
Enjoys Flying

*

Men, Women and
Children

*

The Most Delightful
Experience of a
Lifetime

*

DON'T MISS IT!

H. ROY WAITE, Licensed Pilot.

Students
Trained

Flying Daily
Weather Permitting

*

Finest Flying Field
in New England

*

Safe and Sane
Flying Only

*

'Phone Saugus 8002

Aviation poster for H. Roy Waite, Cliftondale, Massachusetts

The promoters of Revere Beach had contacted Al Valliere and made arrangement with him to supply some night flights over the beach to attract crowds. Night flying was still a novelty, actually flying day or night was still pretty new and exciting. Some of the stunts were not just exciting they were dangerous and many times fatal. Why we never got into real trouble with the Revere display is still a mystery to me. We would have broken every rule in the book had there been any just to attract attention.

Because our show was a night event, flares were attached to the trailing edge of the Jenny's wings. One Niagara Falls flare was mounted on the end of each rib. Remember, we had linen covered, doped wings and fuselage. The dope was a substance making the linen covering tight and reasonably waterproof. The planes finish coat of paint was applied over the dope. One slight mistake and the whole thing would burst into flame like a giant torch. Anyway, we lighted the flares and did modified aerobatics, even loops, with fire and smoke illuminating our every move. It was spectacular. The crowds roared their approval as they stared skyward in the late summer darkness. By the way, those flares were rigged by the photographer/pilot, Harry Jenkins at home on his basement floor. His father would have had his hide had he known what was going on.

Each night that we were scheduled to put on a show "Buster" Brown took one of us along to man the Pyrene fire extinguisher just in case trouble developed. Who ever was left behind in Saugus waited for the returning Jenny to buzz the field, then he would turn on the headlights of the assembled cars so the pilot could see to land.

In the summer of 1921, when I was still with Al in Saugus, there was to be a celebration of some sort at Lake Quanapowett in Wakefield. A parachutist was to make a jump into the lake as part of the festivities. Dick Twombly, the jumper, was a friend of mine and I knew that he couldn't swim a stroke but this was to be his stunt so an inflated inner tube was secured around his waist to keep him afloat when he hit the water. My job this time was to hire a boat and row out to the spot chosen for the drop, pick up Dick and his chute and get him safely to shore.

It was a beautiful, sunny day and I was early, as I always seem to be. I hired a boat and rowed out on the lake. I rowed and rested, rowed and rested, rowed and rested on my oars. For hours I criss-crossed the lake waiting for the plane and the parachutist. Finally,

H. Roy Waite and Melvin W. Hodgins, student pilot. 1912.

at sunset, exhausted and thoroughly exasperated, I paid for the hired boat, climbed wearily into my car and headed for the Saugus Race track. The reason for the "no show" was quickly evident. Standing on its nose in the dirt track was the Avro, which was to have been used to transport the jumper. On take off the pilot, Harry Lessard, failed to see a Model "T" driving on the right side of the runway. The driver of the car was equally careless, and dreadfully surprised I'm sure, when the right wingtip of the plane caught in the bow of the convertible top of the car and nosed over. Al Valliere swore hotly and declared that this was the last time he would hire a Canadian pilot.

Like every other aviation enthusiast, I followed avidly the circuit of events that involved flying. Any gathering, county fair, flying circus, air meet saw the select group of followers en masse. The county fairs whenever and wherever possible capitalized on this relatively new craze to attract crowds. The Brockton Fair of 1921 was no exception.

The fair personnel had cleared a grassy plot for a landing area. To assist the pilots in locating the spot, a white sheet was spread on the ground as a target.

On the day of the fair "Buster" Brown had flown in and landed. Aboard was Bill Bowen, an experienced parachute jumper. Fortunately they had had no difficulty landing but they had mistakenly chosen a small area of relatively smooth grass for the "field" and not even seen the white sheet nearby. When the time came for the plane to take off a group of us gathered and agreed that Brown alone could probably fly out but that the added weight of a passenger would make departure too dangerous in such a short area.

A great debate ensued but Brown, ignoring our advice, climbed into the plane and Bowen got aboard too. They fastened their safety belts and using every inch of the field and full power attempted to lift off over the rapidly approaching trees. They had just broken ground when the plane banked sharply and, within seconds, crashed into a chicken yard. Brown fell free of the inverted fuselage and sustained a broken leg among other things. Bill Bowen was less fortunate. His safely belt held fast on impact and he was left hanging, head down, with the gasoline running into his mouth and choking him. We had some mighty anxious moments trying to extricate him from the wreckage. Both the men ended up in the hospital and, as always, the salvage was the engine and the wheels.

In a recent discussion with a young friend, David Masson, chief mechanic for Hyannis Aviation, we discussed engines of the 1920s and compared them with the current Cessna. The old engines were strictly gravity feed with the gas tank either in the wing or mounted high up front above the carburetor. We agreed that they were very simple and efficient and far easier to maintain than the present systems.

We got on the subject of photography, which was dear to David's heart. I told him about a friend of mine, Mark Hoague, who was an ingenious chap. I used to accompany him on some of his "field trips." He would locate the various mansions in the Beverly Farms, Manchester, and Magnolia, Massachusetts, area and get the names of the owners. I never did know how he pulled that off. Anyway, we would fly over the area and drop prepared letters to the property owners stating that we had taken a picture of their beautiful and impressive estate from the air. We attached the notes to small parachutes tied with ribbon and weighted with a common lead washer. We suggested that they telephone us to purchase the aerial photos if they so desired. To be honest, we hadn't even taken a camera. Should they call we would fly over and get the pictures for them. That way Mark used no extra film. I guess he did well with the idea for I went with him several times on "bluebird" days to distribute the literature and snap the photographs. I couldn't help suggesting to David that maybe Osterville's Oyster Harbor might be a likely place to start such a project. "Maybe John, he said, but I think that most of that area had already been shot from the air by much more experienced photographers than I."

4

The Rutland Fair 1922

•

I had finally become an accessible cog in the wheels of aviation. As such I was much in demand as a mechanic and, as a result, was chosen by Al Valliere for an important assignment. I was to accompany the famous Reverend Belvin W. Maynard, the original "Flying Parson," to Rutland, Vermont, to maintain the plane that was scheduled to carry passengers at the state fair. Mrs. Valliere, wife of the owner of the Avro biplane we were to use, was expecting a child momentarily and felt that flying to Rutland was too risky for her husband. He, therefore, drove his car to Rutland with spare wheels, a propeller and all the bulky parts that might require repair or replacement. I carried only small thing, such as spark plugs, shock cord, and tools in the plane.

The flight up was uneventful. We had only two forced landings, one to replace two faulty sparkplugs and the other to reinforce the landing gear with shock cord for it was too fragile for landing on rough terrain.

Parson Maynard, an ordained Baptist minister and a man of character, was dependable and an excellent pilot. He had been a student at Wake Forest Theological Seminary and enlisted as a private at the close of school in June 1917. He won his wings as a reserve military aviator and was designated to test fly all aircraft shipped to France for assembly there before turning them over to the flight commander. His skill was such that he won acclaim in Romorantin, France, doing more than 318 consecutive loop the loops without losing altitude—an exceptional feat in any plane but truly amazing in the planes of that era. At the time of our trip to Rutland Reverend and Mrs. Maynard were expecting their fourth child.

The *Lynn Daily Evening Item* had obligingly taken a picture of the group of the five of us, Dick Trombley, Harry Jenkins, Reverend Maynard, me, and Al Valliere, in that order left to right,

Lynn Daily Evening Item *photograph of Ed Trombley, parachutist, Harry Jenkins, photographer, the Reverend Belvin Maynard, pilot, John Polando, mechanic, and Al Valliere, ship's owner.*

and printed it just before our departure for the fair. It was a very nice gesture.

The Rutland Fair attracts people from miles around. The fair grounds have permanent buildings and grandstands right in town. By the time the Parson and I arrived, the Ferris wheel was erected, the vendors were setting up their wares, and there was a hum of activity everywhere. A landing area had been mowed on the south side of the barns and all was in readiness for the crowds.

This was a new adventure to me. The excitement of the flight and the change of water and food and I was a bit queasy—not my usual energetic self. The parson, however, was as chipper as always and eager to get the show on the road. To draw the customers, it was his habit to do a little aerial work—a few spins, a loop or two, a steep bank and climb—just a small sample to show that he could thrill an audience when in full performance. Normally an invitation to be part of the act would have delighted me. Today I accepted the invitation reluctantly.

We were aloft only a few minutes when I became nauseated. A spin or two and I was in real trouble. By the time we landed I was violently ill and was immediately banished to the nearby barn.

"Stay out of sight," he shouted. "You'll scare away the customers." Like seasickness, airsickness passes pretty quickly but I had to be told to "get lost" only once.

The next day when Al Valliere arrived, I was sent in a borrowed Model "T" on the ferry to Ticonderoga across the lake for a fifty gallon drum of naptha, our usual fuel. All went well enough until the large drum was dropped behind the driver's seat of the little Ford. There was no other place to put it so I didn't complain but every little bump on the road dropped the drum deeper into the rear area. When I finally arrived back at the fair ground the drum was wedged in so tightly that I was pinned between the steering wheel and the back of the seat and could hardly get out. It took a lot of cussing and maneuvering to free the drum. As usual it was all my fault.

In addition to this being my first long flight, I was to have the singular distinction of doing my first wingwalk. You can imagine my anxiety and nervousness just thinking about it. Little did I know that what was going to happen would be even harder to face than the wingwalking.

Flyers were and are a close knit group. There is a camaraderie that excludes non-flyers. The longer I live the more I realize that flyers communicate best with others in aviation. Our ties are closest to those who have experienced the same things we have experienced. It is a brotherhood.

Shortly after the opening of the fair, and much to the amazement and delight of the parson, Norman Wood, a fellow aviator and buddy from World War I, elbowed his way through the crowd. Wood and his mechanic, Louis Beyette, had flown in from Ticonderoga, New York, unaware that the parson was to be part of the show. A celebration was in order and what better way than to put on a demonstration for their audience.

The three climbed into Al Valliere's Avro and took off. The show was splendid. There were banks, loops and, as a finale, a spin. It started from high in the clear blue sky and was beautiful. The Avro spun, and spun, and spun rapidly losing altitude until the audience gasped. The only problem was that the skill of the pilot was not enough and the plane spun right into the ground killing all three men. Only the victims could have told you what went wrong. As a bystander, I have always felt that the excess weight of the passengers, both large men, jammed the controls and made recovery

*Crash of Avro with the
Reverend Maynard and passengers at Rutland Fair September 7, 1921.*

impossible. We rushed to the wreckage and clawed our way through the rubble of linen, wire and wood to extricate the men but to no avail. I carried the parson to the hospital in my arms in the ambulance but he must have died on impact.

Lieutenant Colonel Harry Jenkins, retired, sent me a very short film clip not too many years ago showing me clawing away with a hammer in my frantic efforts to get the pilot and passengers free of the wreckage. I didn't even know that the pictures had been taken.

Disaster had struck once but the day was young and there were more horrors in store for the audience. A parachute jump from a hot air balloon was scheduled. The jumper, "Daredevil" Smith from Boston, was another friend of mine. Shortly before his ascent he told me, jokingly I thought, that he was going to "cut" three chutes or die trying.

The gimmick was to pull a succession of parachutes, red, white and blue. The drop from the balloon went without a hitch and the red chute blossomed perfectly. That one was cut loose and the white chute opened right on cue. That too was cut free. The third and final parachute, the blue one, failed to open in spite of Smith's frantic efforts to shake it free. Poor Smith plummeted to earth and buried himself in the soft dirt of a flower garden in a private yard near the fair grounds. I was told he broke every bone in his body and I held him in my arms on the way to the now too familiar hospital.

Disaster was not reserved for the performers on that fateful day. A lady became so upset after the accidents that she fell backward from the grandstand and broke her neck. The marshall of the fair was directing traffic in the parking lot when a pickup truck with a long length of pipe backed into him striking him in the throat. According to newspaper accounts, he was paralyzed by the blow and subsequently died of his injuries.

The news of the tragedies reached the newsroom at the *Lynn Daily Evening Item* and it published the picture which they had taken the day the parson and I had left to go to the fair. The headlines announced that the intrepid airmen had been killed. My family was horrified. Knowing nothing of the picture and the article in the *Item* I returned home to an unbelieving family. After a joyful reunion there were demands that I give up flying forever or be disowned. This was, of course, unthinkable. Each of these terrible incidents convinced that I must continue. I would not and could not give up flying. It was only a matter of a few weeks until I signed up with the Massachusetts Air Guard, one of the best moves I ever made but with which my family was most distressed.

In May 1981 I was to meet the man who had been a mechanic for the "Flying Parson" before I was. He presented me with a photocopy of a program for a flying show held November 19, 1922 for the benefit of Mrs. Maynard and her children. The various committees had members such as Colonel Theodore Roosevelt, Cornelius W. Wickersham, and Casey Jones. The list of pilots performing included such greats as Eddie Rickenbacher, Bert Acosta, Lawrence Sperry, and thirty-seven others who would make their mark again and again in the annals of aviation. I am most indebted to "Slim" Henniker for that program. I did not know about the event because I was a lowly mechanic in New England and the affair was held in New York.

I don't think my wife Dode was quite sure of the accuracy of the account of the fair so long ago until we visited Rutland in 1978. The motel we stayed in was on the east side of the grassy area where we had had the landing strip. The grandstands and out buildings are still there much as they were but much improved since the fair of 1922.

Just to satisfy her curiosity, we visited the local newspaper office. There on microfilm was the account of that dreadful day down to the last gruesome detail. We were provided photocopies of the newspaper account but they have become so faded that they are no longer readable. I inquired also about an incident when two planes collided in mid air when I was flying in Rutland in 1934. She made copies of that account too, but more of that later.

5

The Air Guard

•

Formed in 1921 the Air Guard was an unbelievable opportunity for a lot of the young men like me who were interested in aviation but financially unable to attend aviation schools to learn and qualify as mechanics and pilots. Some of the finest mechanics and aviators I know had their initial training in the Guard. Many have remained in the service for thirty years or more and are now pensioners from my old unit.

In the beginning the weekly sessions were held in the Arlington Street Armory in Boston every Friday night. The enlistees were an eager, dedicated bunch who appreciated the opportunity to work on and learn about airplanes. The auditorium was rigged so that the planes could be hoisted up under the roof rafters leaving the floor clear for drills and other activities. A Newport and a Spad were provided for work and demonstration. The major problem was not in getting men to attend the sessions. They were so involved and loved it so that the difficulty lay in trying to dismiss them when the drills were over.

Around 1923 the Massachusetts Air Guard was moved to Framingham State Police School with Curtis Moffatt as the commanding officer. We now had a Hisso Jenny to experiment on and our expanded facilities included a grass field. There were also six civilian planes and two or three army planes at Framingham.

The requirements were much the same as they are now. We had one weekend each month on duty and a summer encampment for two weeks. If I remember correctly, our first two-week tour of duty with the Guard was in the summer of 1923. We took the train from Boston to New York then proceeded to Mitchell Field where we were billeted.

Mitchell Field at that time had a compound of prisoners of war who were doing daily labor. They were housed and fed in an area

Above and opposite page: Air Guard en route to Langley Field, Norfolk, Virginia, for summer camp. 1925.

separated from our mess hall/tent by only a heavy wire fence. True to my nature, I managed to get myself in hot water immediately.

As part of our rations, we were each given one orange. I had had enough chow and couldn't have cared less about the orange. The POWs were obviously treated with less consideration so I decided, on a whim, to roll my orange through the fence to the poor devils. The sight of that bright orange rolling rapidly across the grass and under the wire barrier brought chuckles from the guardsmen but, as it passed under the fence, a riot ensued. The prisoners fell on that hapless orange and, in the scramble, all you could see was flying legs and arms as every man tried to snag the orange for himself. There were fistfights, real knock-down, drag-out variety. The next few days saw me sweeping walks and retrieving butts with a constant military escort watching my every move.

ELLY   POLANDO   J.J. KELLY   PAT CROZIER
CONNOR   MEMBRINO

LANGLEY FIELD VA. 1925

Air Guard duty at Langley Field. 1925.

I had just gotten back on my regular duties when a baseball
game was organized. When I came up to bat the pitcher, an officer.
threw a beanball at me that grazed the back of my head. My instant
reaction was retaliation. I let the bat fly. The pitcher jumped but not
soon enough and the bat struck his leg a nasty blow. Not too chagrined, I explained that it was an accident and, fortunately for me,
they bought the story so I was spared further disciplinary action.

In 1925 we took the coastal steamship from Boston to Newport
News, Virginia, for our two week encampment. Here we shared the
facilities at Langley Field with a lighter-than-air group to which I
was temporarily assigned. One of our various jobs was to grasp the
mooring lines of the clumsy observation balloons. I had had a bit of
experience in the field of hot air ballooning as you have read. One
chap, in an attempt to do a really good job, I assume, wrapped the
mooring line around his wrist. Can you imagine what would have
happened to him if the balloon had lifted off with him dangling

Alphonse Valliere, John Polando, Mark Hogue, and Harry J. Jenkins. 1924.

from a shroud line by one hand? For once I made the right choice and I told him about his error before he met with disaster.

For some years after that, we made our summer encampment at Marstons Mills on what is now known as the Cape Cod Airport and presently run by Harry and Rick Kornheiser. Here we pitched tents in neat rows and swam in the nearby lake for recreation and bathing.

The highlights of those tours of duty were the picnic baskets of goodies that our families brought to us on the Sunday visitor's days. It was a good thing they did. Military mess was almost inedible at times. Fortunately, the mechanics were better at their chosen vocation than were the men assigned to the cook tent or we would have been in real trouble.

I enjoyed my duty with the Massachusetts National Guard which became the Air National Guard. I attained the rank of sergeant but had to resign from the Guard when leaving the country. On my return I was advised that I would have to begin as a buck private again. This didn't appeal to me so I didn't rejoin.

6
Forced Landing
•

I now had several years of expert, and inexpert, training and experience in aircraft engines and airframes. Planes were in the development stage and repairs were unending. The landing strips were few and far between. More often than not they were just relatively smooth, grassy area. From the moment the ships were airborne, the cautious pilots were on the alert for possible places to set down in case of emergencies of which there were many. I was constantly summoned to rescue and repair downed planes, not necessarily for my extraordinary skills but for my enthusiastic response to a call for help. I'd go anywhere, anytime to help a flyer in need.

One incident was particularly notable. A forced landing on Long Beach in Gloucester resulted in a hurried and harried call to me for aid. Because there was no easy way of hauling a plane that had a forced landing up the steep embankment, I was asked to switch engines right on the beach which was not too far from the drawbridge in the heart of town.

Night was falling by the time my helper and I arrived at Long Beach, so it was necessary to park the truck facing the nose of the plane and work by the light of the headlamps. Work had just about begun when a man with a soft hat pulled low over his eyes walked up and asked us to put out the headlights. We explained our dilemma and said we had been told to switch engines as quickly as possible before the rising tide made departure impossible. The intruder was unimpressed with our problem. He had problems of his own and he quickly convinced us of his priority by patting a holster and gun in his belt. His orders were that we disappear and not return to the beach until daylight.

At the crack of dawn we were back on the beach in time to see piles of wooden cases of liquor that had been dropped by a rumrunner at night during high tide. There was a bucket brigade extending from the low water mark up the steep banking to one of the large houses on the bluff. The men were handing up cases with incredible speed in their efforts to avoid detection. A case of Gordon's gin, minus one broken bottle, was our reward for obedience. Then we set to work and switched the engine so the pilot could get off on the next low tide.

7

My Jenny

·

It was 1924 when I bought my one and only airplane, a Jenny and she was a "basket case." The lower wings were gone, the lower longeron was split and one wheel and tires were missing. The OX-5 engine needed some work but was in reasonably good condition.

Thrilled and excited with my $5,000 treasure, I borrowed a truck and set up shop in my father's barn on Franklin Street in Lynn. Because I was employed during the day as an automobile mechanic, I was able to spend only nights and weekends on my own plane. The work was slow but satisfying.

My project was progressing but the barn was ill equipped so, when I landed a job with the Rickenbacker Automobile Agency in Salem, I wheedled permission to put my Jenny in the shop where the tools were readily available. I got permission to work on her evenings and weekends.

All went well until the day the bank that held the mortgage on the agency decided to make an on-premises check for insurance purposes. The dealership papers and insurance were written to cover automobiles, not airplanes, so it was a mad scramble to find a place to hide my toy. Hasty arrangements with the garage across the street saved the day. I am most grateful that the bank representative called to announce his intentions instead of just dropping in.

It took me two years to make the Jenny airworthy. Now, ready for assembly, she was hoisted on a truck and was taken to East Boston Airport. The Air Guard had moved its operations to the airport from the Framingham location and had its own hangar and shop on the airport facility.

With the approval of our commanding officer, Paul Rouillard, Wally Holbrook and I did the final assembly and tune-up on the Jenny. Neither of us had yet soloed, so Julian Dexter volunteered to

The Jenny, John's only airplane, after the crash in Weston, Massachusetts, 1926.

test-fly her. The check ride proved her sound and airworthy. Now she was finally ready for hire.

The first job for the Jenny was a stunt. A Harvard student, on a wager, hired the Jenny to fly him over the golf course in Weston. He was going to make a parachute jump and "drop in" on his father, who was playing golf that day. Julian was to fly to Weston and pick up his passenger while I drove over to give him a hand.

Julian Dexter had been flying a Hisso Jenny, which had a cruising speed of ninety miles per hour. My Jenny with an OX-5 cruised at about sixty-five miles per hour. This difference in horsepower was to prove insurmountable.

On takeoff from Weston, Dexter misjudged the speed and lift and hooked the wing section in a tree. Except for the engine and wheels, nothing was left of my beloved plane. With her fuselage broken behind the wing section, she was a total loss. Financed on a shoestring she had no insurance. My original cost of $5,000 plus the expense of parts for repair and two years of labor went down the drain in a matter of seconds. The salvaged engine was worth about $2,000 but that was small comfort. All my investment in love, labor and money was gone. Thank goodness Julian and his passenger were unharmed.

8

Russell Boardman and Weston Fire

•

In the summer of 1923 on an outing at Revere Beach Amusement Park I met Russell Boardman, who was to completely change my self-image, my lifestyle and my goals.

Russell was a dashing, delightful fellow in his mid-twenties. Born to a Connecticut farm family, he was early to leave home and quick to learn the polish and presence that set him apart from the crowd. He was afraid of nothing. He would try anything that required daring and he always, or almost always, came up grinning and looking for another challenge.

At the time when Russell and I met, he was racing a motorcycle in a silodrome partly for money, partly for thrills, partly because almost no one else was foolhardy enough to run around the perpendicular walls of the silo. To add to the excitement, a girl was riding on the handlebars. The roar of the cycle in the small area was deafening. The higher he climbed on the walls, the better the audience like it, and Russell loved pleasing the crowd. In fact, just a couple of nights before we met Russell had overstepped his limitations and had whipped out over the top of the silo wall and dropped to the ground, motorcycle, girl and all in one great heap. Miraculously no one was seriously hurt and the bike had not been badly damaged.

Always in search of adventure, I was captivated by what I saw. As long as Russell performed in Revere I was his constant companion and admirer. From cycles to airplanes was an easy and natural progression for Russell.

During the summer of 1925-26 Russell and I operated a shop in Weston, Massachusetts. We were using World War I surplus airplanes. Most of the ships were still in their original wooden crates and all had been sold to us "as is." They were made of wood and fabric and the years had taken their toll. The frames were still sound but the fabric was so rotten that the frames had to be stripped and

Russell Norton Boardman

recovered with linen. It was a long, laborious job removing all the fabric and recovering, doping and painting them again. As I am sure your recall, the dope was a type of sizing that sealed the linen fabric from weather and shrank the fabric tight to the frame.

The first plane to be completed was sold to Ray Broadhurst. It was powered by my salvaged OX-5 engine. There was great jubilation when we finally finished the job. Payment was to be received upon delivery the next day. We gave the shop a final check then stood back to admire our project before locking up. We had been exceedingly careful to leave nothing flammable uncovered, no lights were left on and no equipment plugged into the outlets. We

John Polando's one wheel landing. 1927.

had made sure of that before closing down. We never found out what happened during the night but a fire started in the hangar and consumed everything, including Ray Broadhurst's plane. Earl Boardman, Russell's brother, had financed the operation. My first meeting with Earl was to deliver the devastating news of the fire. We were, as usual, unable to afford the luxury of insurance so Earl advised us to abandon the project.

My close contacts with aviators and airplanes since 1920 have given me an excellent foundation and insight into aviation. I had been exposed to a great variety of problems in which I was obliged to analyze, improvise and often "invent" solutions. In many cases the word "invent" was most accurate. There were situations where no one had any prior experience so we devised answers to the problem. Consequently, when I had an opportunity to go for a check ride in someone else's plane I was eager to accept because I picked up pointers on the mechanics of flying.

Many of the pilots at East Boston Airport took me flying with them. Most let me take the controls in flight but reserved the complexities of takeoff and landing for themselves. Some of the pilots, perhaps a little unsure of themselves or their passenger, took me up only with the stipulation that my hands grasp the visible edge of the cockpit at all times. A. Ponton "Bonbon" deArce and Windsor "Mike" Harlow were two of the most able pilots at East Boston, and they shared the dubious honor of polishing my technique. Mike gave me about two and a half hours of instruction, then graciously, told Bonbon that I knew as much as he did. I doubt that his assessment was accurate for he had a grand total of sixty-seven hours to his credit at that time according to his old log book. In their capable hands I soloed in three and a half hours in an OX-5 Eaglerock. But, as any pilot will readily tell you, that is the beginning of the beginning. From that hour a pilot is constantly learning the fine points of flying. My Christmas gift to myself in 1927 was my solo flight. What a marvelous gift, with what unforeseen adventures to savor.

The planes of that era had limited instrumentation. The aircraft themselves were fragile and parts were always breaking, fraying, rotting, or falling off.

Speaking of falling off, on the day I got my private license and with thirteen hours total flying time, I lost a wheel on takeoff. The procedure under such circumstances was for one of the mechanics to run on the field, attract the attention of the pilot of the damaged aircraft then hold a wheel up on the right side, if this was the missing wheel, and on the left side if the wheel was missing on the left.

The day of my mishap there was some confusion. Two mechanics appeared almost simultaneously and, waving frantically, each held up a wheel, one on my left side and one on my right side. My immediate and devastating conclusion was that I had lost both wheels on takeoff. By the time the ground crew got organized, I had visualized a belly landing on the not too smooth dirt beside the cinder runway. Happily, only the left wheel was gone. Gently, very gently I eased the plane down, fearing the worst, but I managed to bring her to a stop damaging only one wingtip. The Boston papers made much of my success. Just a short time before my mishap, Charles Lindbergh had had a similar problem in Texas but had cracked up on landing.

East Boston Airport was growing steadily. Originally we had one "T" shaped cinder runway and one hangar. Then there were three hangars. The dredges were pulling up harbor silt and depositing it along the gritty, marshy shoreline. The faster they dredged the more rapidly the field grew. The proximity to the city of Boston prompted the speed with which the facility was built.

The craze for flying grew as the field expanded. There was the Harvard Flying Club made up in part of Augie Pabst, Henry Timkin, Maxfield Parrish, Jr., and Crocker Snow. These young men were wealthy and aviation was the newest thrill. Girls gathered in droves around the helmeted, leather jacketed crowd. The Harvard Yale games were a mini flyin. The flying was mostly serious but the atmosphere was definitely party. Perhaps the most expensive and exciting birthday gift received by any of the boys was the Tri Motor Ford given to Henry Timkin. It was the only one at East Boston and dwarfed everything else on the field.

During the 1920s I spent most of my waking hours with my first love—aviation, but I did manage a modest social life as long as it didn't infringe on the flying.

I had enjoyed the company of lots of girls but in 1926 I met Millie Bradshaw, a pretty, young blond widow with a small daughter, Marjorie. Several factors, as I see it now, were involved in my decision to marry her. First, my mother was dead set against it; second, Millie needed someone to support her and Marjorie; and third, someone else was courting her at the time. I won. We were married and went on a short honeymoon. We made the rounds of airport and visited a host of my flying friends. I had a great time but Millie didn't take too kindly to that sort of honeymoon. I'm afraid that I was more than a little unmindful and insensitive to her wishes then and, I guess, the whole of our married life.

We had lots of happy times, too, and in 1928 we had a son, John, Jr. Unfortunately, my career in aviation did not lend itself to family life. My hours were terrible I must admit. I worked nights, Saturdays, Sundays, and holidays. In emergencies, and all families have a few, I was rarely there. It was a difficult life for Millie. If she invited guests for dinner, I frequently did not make the party. Often I could barely find the makings for a late sandwich when I finally got home in the wee hours of the morning. With reluctance, we split up in the mid 1930s after my trip to Turkey and the fiasco in Calcutta, India. To be truthful, it was more my fault than Millie's, but I didn't realize it at the time. I was so engrossed in my own commitments that everything else was secondary.

9

Flying in Florida

•

In 1929 I flew for Jack Crane. We had two planes, a J-65 Travel Air, which I flew, and a Keystone Commuuter amphibian which Jack flew. Jack's employer was a wealthy New Yorker by the name of McCarthy who wintered in Florida. He was an aviation enthusiast so, for the winter months, we flew all over the state of Florida.

One incident I remember well was when Jack landed the Keystone Commuter at Palm Beach and taxied onto the sand to admire the bathing beauties and, of course, to be admired by them. As luck would have it, the landing gear didn't lock properly. Actually it was the right strut which malfunctioned. Anyway, the girls he was trying to impress and some other sunbathers who had gathered were obliged to push him back into the water where he could retract the gear. He took off then landed in the water at Miami where repairs were made, thanks to Juan Trippe, president of PanAm Airways.

We had been based at Drew Field, Tampa. All of Mr. McCarthy's friends and associates, as well as Jack's friends, were given rides. From Tampa we moved our operation, if you can call it that, to Miami. Florida in 1929 was quite different from the Florida we know now. There were broad expanses of undeveloped Everglades. We were warned to follow the Tamiami Trail so that, if we were forced down, we would have a chance of survival. There were lots of alligators in those lonely stretches and the possibility of finding a downed plane in the heavy undergrowth was slim.

The Keystone Commuter that Jack flew had an Achilles' Heel. Its exhaust system was engineered to emit up over the leading edge of the wing where a metal strip was mounted to protect the fabric but the plane wouldn't start in a crosswind, so, if overloaded with fuel, it would give off a flash of flames. We found that out when Jack was in just such a situation and burned off the wings. We had to dismantle the ship and send it back to Boston for repairs.

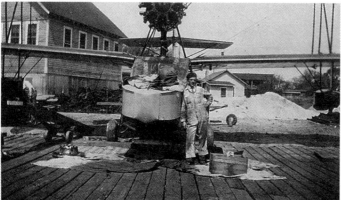

*Jack Crane, Mr. McCarthy and John in Florida with Keystone Commuter
1929 after wings were destroyed by fire and then were repaired.*

After the social season was over, Mr. McCarthy requested that I
go to Hicksville, New York, where Jack and I would test fly a
Curtiss Wright experimental aircraft. I had been gone from home
so long that I begged off and returned instead to Lynn. A couple of
days later the newspapers had an account of the crash of the trainer
that I was supposed to have flown. It stated that both occupants, the
pilot, Jack Crane, and his passenger, Mr. McCarthy had been killed.

10

Floyd Bennett to Istanbul, Turkey

•

I had never lost contact with Russell Boardman, although he had spent months at a time in Arizona. He and his brother, Earl, had a place in Flagstaff called Rim Rock Ranch. Russell was in charge of the operations there.

Russ did a lot of flying, some wing walking, and stunt flying, acquiring skills known to only a select few pilots and stuntmen from California. Many of the Hollywood stars enjoyed the luxury of owning and flying their own planes. One of the most popular stars of that day was Wallace Beery, who was an exceptional pilot and a good friend of Russell's. Russell was in his glory. He was an extremely handsome, well mannered, bright, and responsive man and it was seemingly no effort at all for him to rise to the occasion.

In 1925-26, between trips to Arizona, Russell started the Travel Air Agency in the building built and owned by Frederick Lothrope Ames and known as East Coast Aircraft Company, located at East Boston Airport at Jeffrey's Point. It is now called Logan International Airport. Russell made tours of New England in the airplane *Arabella* using an old-fashioned telephone—the upright kind—as a microphone to broadcast from the ship in flight. It was an advertising stunt that worked out pretty well. I was working in the same general location at the Wright Engine Agency so we were in regular contact with each other. My connection with Wright engines played an important part in our adventure with the Bellanca, then named the *American Legion*, which Russ bought in 1930.

By 1929 Russell was contemplating a record breaking flight. So were many others, as the records will attest. What record Russ would challenge was still under consideration, but he was moving even then toward preparing himself for the competition. With large sums of money being offered for record breaking flights many

Russell with the Bellanca, American Legion, *to be renamed the* Cape Cod.

were eager to make their mark in the field of aviation. Most flights were transatlantic but prizes were awarded for high altitude, long distance, endurance, and other records worthy of recognition.

In the summer of 1930 Russell bought the Bellanca, the *American Legion* which he renamed the *Cape Cod.* By now the general feeling with the aviation community was one of excitement. Existing records were being challenged in every category. One of the major problems was that many of the attempts were made without proper preparation. This was suicidal. Even with meticulous care you were subject to weather variations as well as frequent mechanical difficulties that resulted in placing them off target or they were listed as missing and presumed dead. The books are full of the accounts of pilots who disappeared without a trace. It was a terrible waste of men and machines and, eventually, officials cracked down on the number of permits granted. One of the lucky

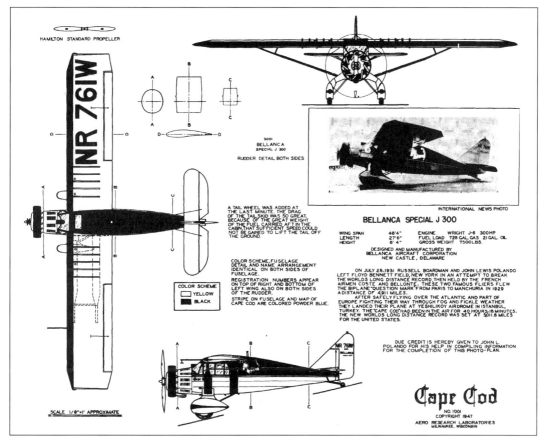

Specifications for Cape Cod, NR 761W.

ones was "Wrong Way" Corrigan who simply outsmarted the powers that be and made a successful, if undeclared, Atlantic crossing. My reference books do not now mention his name.

We were still having minor problems with the Bellanca and Russell had not decided what record he would attempt to break. Then we had an unfortunate accident. We were gassing up when the right wing caught fire. Before we could put it out it had burned the covering off the wing completely and burned much of the fabric off the right side of the fuselage. In deep despair, we called Mr. Bellanca at Wilmington, Delaware, and were instructed to disassemble the plane and truck her to him at the factory. I volunteered to drive the truck myself. I didn't trust anyone to care for her as Russell or I would. It was October 1930 and getting much too late

Cape Cod *after fueling accident burned the fabric off one wing and the fuselage. October 1930.*

in the season to even contemplate an Atlantic crossing.

The repairs were completed in late November but winter weather was upon us making us look far into 1931 before we could even consider a record breaking flight. We had, by now, decided on the long-distance record, challenging Coste and Bellonte's record from Paris to Manchuria, a distance of 4911 miles. This decision was reached with the help of Sandy Lewis of the Department of Commerce, who suggested that theirs was a record as yet unbroken. We had fuel capacity sufficient to get to Rome, which had been our original destination but, as one friend put it, "You won't even get your name in the paper if you go to Rome" and he was right.

With our proposed destination Istanbul, Turkey, we were again to consult with our friend, Mr. Bellanca. Additional fuel would be needed to complete a flight of such distance. Mr. Ballance's reply was typical of him. "We fix," he said and he did.

As soon as the word got out about Russell's plans he was bombarded with requests to be part of the adventure. To settle the matter he turned to me saying, "Johnnie, how much do you weigh." "About 127 pounds," I replied. "You'll do." That was our only discussion regarding his choice of companions.

Reams have been written about the famous flight to Turkey on July 28-30, 1931. Nothing has quite conveyed the real suspense and personal commitment that faced us as fathers and husbands. No one said anything about our families and the apprehension and anger they felt. We owed much to them and their patience under very trying circumstances. To be totally honest, Russ and I would have done it with or without their blessing. That they tried to understand is certainly to their credit.

By 1931, the Atlantic had been crossed east to west, west to east and northeast to southwest. In 1930 alone, nine outstanding records had been set. In view of the fact that so many flights had taken place but few had actually landed at their original target, we decided to declare our intentions before departure. Russell stated flatly that we were going to Istanbul, Turkey, a distance of roughly 4999 miles. That was a slim, slim margin if we were wholly successful in our attempt, for one must exceed the previous record by at least one hundred kilometers, a distance of eighty-two miles, to be credited with a new record.

Now, finally committed, we had some interesting problems to solve before our departure: namely, we had to dispose of the empty fuel tins that would provide our additional supply of gas. For several days we flew over New York harbor practicing. I would open the window, hold out an empty can and tap Russell on the knee. He would push forward on the stick so that the can flew harmlessly beneath the elevators. Only once in our actual flight did the can hit the stabilizer, scaring us out of wits but doing no visible damage. In that case the handle had broken off in the slipstream so the can itself was gone before I touched Russell's knee.

The fuel problem solved, other things plagued us. We had a fixed pitch Hamilton Standard propeller. This meant that we must decide the pitch that we could live with for takeoff and distance before we departed. That was really fine tuning. We developed 300 horsepower at 2000 revolutions per minute. To flatten the pitch to

Preparation for departure showing Russell Boardman, John Polando,
Guiseppi Bellanca, Dr. Kimball, Clyde Pangborn, and Hugh Herndon
with the Cape Cod.

1800 RPMs on the ground robbed us of air speed so we played with
settings. We found that at 1650 RPM we would be using about 65
percent power. Less than that would make it impossible to get off
the ground.

The artificial horizon was operated by a venturi tube hung on
the side of the fuselage. Now it is operated by a vacuum pump. The
instrument was six to seven inches long and would not fit on the
instrument panel so I mounted it in front of the windshield and had
an aluminum hood and gasket made to protect it from the weather.
As it turned out, it only operated five or six hours, did a 180, and
ceased to function.

When you talk about being prepared, Russell contacted a
caterer, a Mr. Tony Argon, in October 1930 requesting that he have
a lunch of roast chickens, sandwiches, fruit, and lots of coffee ready

for us on an hour's notice. Whether Tony Argon was our caterer in July 1931 I don't remember but the menu did not change even if the supplier did.

Dr. James Henry Kimball, instructor of meteorology for the U.S. Army in 1917-18 and later principal meteorologist for the United States Weather Bureau until his death in 1943, was to us and all the aspiring aviators the single most important person of all for he had the last word on the weather. Everyone departing from the United States deferred to his superior judgment and predictions. Hence when Wiley Post and Harold Gatty departed it was with Dr. Kimball's blessing and Russell's and my help. When they returned eight days later Russell and I were there to greet them and congratulate them on their successful round the world flight.

It was five o'clock in the morning of July 24 that we made our first attempt at departure. We were able to clear the power lines on Flatbush Avenue, courtesy of the power company and their crew who had laid them flat for us, but we were unable to climb due to the overload of fuel. We were flying between the tall buildings of Brooklyn and, finally, in desperation, Russell and I agreed to dump five hundred gallons of the precious fuel on sleeping Brooklyn and return to Floyd Bennett Field to await another day. We later learned that a trail of fire followed the plane as we touched down. I had failed to entirely close the fourteen-inch dump valve and fuel was leaking from the tank and was ignited by the tailskid when it touched the runway. Only the propeller wash saved us from catching the *Cape Cod* on fire.

Our original plan had been to leave from Roosevelt Field but, effective May 23, 1931, Floyd Bennett Field made its new hot top runway available to all of us. It was far better than the grass strip at Roosevelt Field so we all availed ourselves of this rare opportunity.

As a result of the difficulty with our first departure, I decided that the tail skid should be modified. By splitting the skid and mounting a ball-bearing wheel from a mobile metal cart into the skid, we eliminated some of the drag. If we were unfortunate enough to make a second unsuccessful attempt to go we had at least eliminated the danger of setting ourselves on fire.

Actually, the dump valve I had failed to shut completely was a safety feature that Mr. Bellanca had developed. If you must land in the water, first dump your fuel, then close the valve and you can, presumable, float for several days. One man is known to have floated for three days due to the buoyancy of the empty tanks. He was finally picked up by a Shell Oil tanker. He was, incidentally, using Shell fuel. Quite a coincidence.

Our second try was at the same hour on July 28. Our take off was frightful. We lifted off, then settled back several times before finally becoming airborne. We broke ground on the parking area between the hangars thirty-five to forty yards beyond the end of the runway and less than thirty yards from the highway. I learned years later that Earl Boardman, who had taken off immediately behind us, looked with dismay at the fuel streaming from the trailing edge of the wings via the overflow vents. He made no sign to us that anything was amiss. Instead, he flew alongside us giving us encouragement and confidence up the coast until we were well north of Boston. Only then did he return to New York to take care of the details of our departure.

The flight north and east was relatively uneventful. The sky was clear and we had no difficulty identifying the familiar landmarks. We had both flown over every inch of the checkpoints as far north as the northern tip of Maine, so we knew the area by heart. Beyond that the rocky coastline was easily visible and, I might add, a comforting sight as we headed for Cape Race, Newfoundland. Here we circled the lighthouse, dropped one of our *New York Times* newspapers with its small parachute, and headed east over the great Atlantic. The *New York Times* considered it good advertising, I guess, so supplied us sufficient newspapers to make three drops and still have some left to present to Mustfa Kemal Pasha if we succeeded in completing our flight. They paid us $2500 for doing it.

Prior to our departure, Russ and I had spent many evenings studying with a navigator. The great circle route chosen was plotted carefully. We flew designated compass headings for a specific number of hours, changing directions as indicated on our chart. Our magnetic compass was one of the few functioning instruments and we never deviated from our original plan. The Sperry directional gyro worked perfectly; the air speed needle and ball were fine. We had been supplied with flares, which we were to drop from the window of the plane onto the surface of the water below. We were then to adjust for drift by checking the direction of the smoke from the flares. We had a Pioneer drift indicator mounted in the floor of the cockpit to check the drift. That was a great idea, but the cloud cover was so thick that we flew at twelve thousand feet and never saw the water in the entire crossing.

The only problem we encountered with the magnetic compass was that each time we emptied a gas can into the tank, the needle swung around. Once, in fact, we found we had made a 180 degree turn and were headed west. This was easily rectified but a bit disconcerting as we had no point of reference and had to rely wholly on our compass reading.

The first glimpse of earth was on the morning of July 29. We spotted a break in the overcast and down below saw a great patch of green. It had to be the most beautiful thing I had ever seen.

Descending through the break in the overcast, we spotted a double trunk railroad which we followed and it took us over the Croydon Airdrome and the majestic city of London. Here too we dropped the *New York Times* newspapers.

The next leg of our journey was far more interesting and exciting for we now were crossing the English Channel and were headed for Paris. Night had fallen by the time we reached LeBourget Field, where we dropped more of the newspapers. This time our aim was a little less accurate and the papers were not found until the next morning after daybreak. The City of Paris, her sparkling lights and her legends, faded from sight as we turned in a more easterly direction toward the mountains south of Munich, Germany.

By now all the auxiliary gas cans had been used and thrown overboard. The cushions that were our seats on the hot oil tanks had been held out the windows and mercifully cooled a dozen times. We had drunk black coffee until the "relief containers" were filled with a frightening black fluid. Russ had lost one of the containers when he held it out the window to dump it and we got drenched with the foul black stuff. The two roast chickens and the sandwiches had hardly been touched. Our knees had stopped knocking at last, but we were so keyed up that food was not too appealing. Sitting in one position for such a length of time does strange things to the body. The aching muscles were almost unbearable. No one had given us any inkling of the physical agony of prolonged flight without being able to move. Charles Lindbergh had shaken our hands and wished us success, but he never mentioned that balm for our parched lips and some kind of muscle relaxant for our aching limbs should be part of our equipment. In lieu of liniment, we rubbed toothpaste on our swollen knees. I doubt that the medication was any help but rubbing did improve the circulation somewhat.

By now, we were shouting at each other for the constant drone of the engines had taken its toll and we were partially deaf. Eventually all our ills would be forgotten, but at that particular time they were very real as was the fatigue that was troubling both of us. Russell dropped off to sleep briefly and, in so doing, put forward pressure on the joystick. I was forced, finally, to waken him before we lost too much altitude. Shortly thereafter I dozed. The next thing I knew Russell was shaking me. "You've been asleep half an hour. You look great, must feel rested too," he said. Funny thing is, I really did. I later learned that I had slept possibly five minutes but, like Russ, had fallen forward on the stick forcing the nose of the faithful *Cape Cod* downward.

Our position now was well south of Munich and we were flying at night in the northern fringes of the Bavarian Alps. The mountains rose to a majestic fourteen thousand feet but we could safely maintain an altitude of only twelve thousand. Even then there was danger of icing up. Our only hope was to fly in circles in the dark valleys until daylight, so circle we did for hours. After what seemed an eternity, dawn pierced the darkness and sent its searching rays from the mountain peaks down into the lush green valleys. We were at last freed from our dark prison.

Exhausted as we were, the sun brought wide grins to our unshaven faces. The Danube River was easily distinguishable in the distance, and we followed her to Sophia, Bulgaria, then the Bosporus, and finally, shining, beckoning in the distance, the minarets of Istanbul. The exultation that we experienced at that moment made us forget our weariness, our pain. We had done what no one else had done. We had flown farther, non-stop in a single engine airplane than anyone else in the world. Best, and perhaps most important of all, we would make our destination. Many men had flown the Atlantic but few had made their stated target.

To accommodate the additional fuel needed for our flight, Mr. Ballanca had moved the landing gear back several inches to adjust the center of balance for takeoff. Now, with gas tanks empty, we had the problem of keeping the tail down on landing for the *Cape*

Arrival at Yechilokeuy Airdrome, Istanbul, Turkey, July 30, 1931.
Ambassador Joseph Grew greeting flyers.

Cod was now noticeably nose heavy. I threw thermos bottles, cushions, jackets, anything and everything that was movable into the back of the fuselage. Then, gingerly, I climbed as far back into the frame as I dared to go to help compensate. We both knew that one misstep and I would go through the fabric of the plane. So, with me crouched in the tail of the *Cape Cod*, Russell touched down on the not-too-smooth surface of the Yechilkeuy Airdrome in Istanbul, Turkey, on July 30, 1931, without mishap. Before we taxied up to the waiting delegation Russ made me resume my seat up front.

The first hand that shook mine was that of Ambassador Joseph Grew from the United States. He and his daughter Anita had waited at the airport for several hours. Twice they had headed back to the embassy and twice had second thoughts, if indeed we succeeded in our flight, about the possibility of missing our arrival, and that was unthinkable.

Air traffic was moderately heavy for 1931, so, when we appeared as a tiny speck in the sky, we were presumably one of the regular aircraft on a routine flight. When, however, the speck became clearer, and the bright yellow of the fuselage and the shiny black of the wings was recognizable, our ambassador led his entourage out on the field.

Ambassador Grew's greeting was warm but a bit reserved. The reason was soon evident. "Was it non-stop?" he asked guardedly. "Yes," I answered, puzzled by the question. Then he really glowed. "That's all I wanted to know," he said chuckling, as he helped me unbend my stiffened legs and climb carefully through the window of the plane. We later learned that the wire service had reported, "U.S. Flyers Down, Will Continue" —no names had been given and Grew had feared that we were the flyers mentioned. In fact it was Clyde Pangborn and Hugh Herndon, who were making a routine fuel stop on their round-the-world flight from Floyd Bennett Field. They had departed the same day we had. Our baragraph, installed by Mr. Heinmueller in New York, substantiated our claim a couple of days later. The instrument was removed from the *Cape Cod* and placed in the embassy safe until it could be read by the officials of the Aeronautic Internationale, the only authorized persons to read and record world record flights.

I said we had climbed out the window in the aircraft. That's right: we had no doors, no interior walls or bulkheads, no radio, no

American Ambassador Joseph Grew greeting John and Russell on their arrival.

starter, no brakes, no lights—nothing extra so we could carry every ounce of fuel possible. We were to find out later that our margin of safety on fuel was mighty slim. On our arrival in Istanbul, we had five gallons of gasoline left. Our holding pattern during the night in the mountains had nearly cost us our success. Our fuel gauge was a vertical glass tube. We had discovered to our dismay sometime before we landed that the slightest dip of the wing would empty the gauge. We had no way of knowing that even a missed approach might have left the tanks completely empty.

Like sailors after a long sea voyage, we staggered when we walked and stooped like old men. Our sweaters were so deeply creased that the wrinkles never did come out. We were a pretty drab looking duo.

Ambassador Grew introduced us to the Turkish officials who had arrived at the airport just in time to see us land. There was an honor guard to greet us. We were ushered into the administration building, where an elaborate buffet had been spread on long draped tables in our honor. Here we were toasted in several languages with

Holders of world's record for a non-stop, non-fueling flight - New York to Istanbul, Turkey - 5050 miles in 50 hours - July 28th to 30th, 1931

Russell Boardman and John Polando posing with the Cape Cod.

champagne. The crowd that gathered there seemed as excited as Russell and I were. Fifty years later I was to meet the Honorary Turkish ambassador, Orhan Gunduz, who, as a boy of ten, was at Yeschilkeuy Airdrome on that special day. Everyone was most cordial and gracious, and somehow, language was not an insurmountable barrier. Their enthusiasm and warmth conveyed their message to us eloquently. Fortunately, Ambassador Grew realized how tired we were so he took care of the amenities and whisked us off in his chauffeur driven Buick.

Our next stop was the American embassy, where we were introduced to the staff and posed for photographers. Finally, we headed for the Para Palace Hotel, where we were to occupy the bridal suite as guests of the Turkish Aviation Society.

The timing of our flight was propitious, to say the least, although we had no way of knowing it in advance or, for that matter, changing it if we had. A French aviation squadron was on a propaganda tour of Turkey. Coste and Bellonte, the holders of the world's long distance record from Paris to Manchuria in 1929, were

John Polando and Russell Boardman being introduced to Coste and Bellonte, former long distance record holders.

their "exhibit A" in their attempt to sell the Turkish government French planes for the Turkish air force. Suddenly, two unshaven, uncombed, dirty Americans flew in with a Bellanca aircraft powered by a Wright Whirlwind engine claiming, quietly, that they had just flown farther by at least ninety miles than the Frenchmen. The elegantly uniformed and beribboned Coste and Bellonte were distantly gracious. "We shall wait for confirmation," they said, rather grimly.

We left them to their discomfort and went finally to our rooms. They were absolutely beautiful. We had a sitting room with French doors onto a balcony from which we waved to the crowd of admirers in the street below. Officials actually forbade the blowing of horns or any loud noises of any kind for twenty-four hours while we slept.

Our first priority was, as you can readily imagine, a bath. I made mine lukewarm and shallow. I was afraid I'd fall asleep and drown. Then I crawled into bed expecting to sleep for twenty-four hours or more. Instead I tossed and turned for what seemed hours before dozing off, due I guess to the over stimulation of the past two days and being over tired. Sometime later Russell shook me awake to eat. He had wakened famished and had managed to communicate with the Turkish guard at our door. Much as if he had rubbed Aladdin's magic lamp, the food appeared, enough for a small army, and wine and, unfortunately for them, Turkish cigarettes. We ate, sipped and smoked until, now pretty relaxed, we dropped off to sleep again. In so doing our cigarettes ignited the sofa on which were sitting. The next thing we knew the room was filled with smoke, and we had to get help to put out the fire.

Within a few hours of our arrival and the announcement of our successful trip via the radio and the press, we were inundated with telegrams. They arrived from the president, the politicians, our families, friends, and total strangers. The governor of Massachusetts and the mayors of New York and of Boston all sent telegrams. So had our old friend Bob Stevens. He had been marvelous to us in New York and had, I believe, been one of our financial backers. After our return to the States, he was instrumental in securing the Distinguished Flying Cross for Russell and for me from President Hoover. After World War II he served as Secretary of the Army under President Eisenhower and I had the good fortune to visit him in his office in the Pentagon. The small American flag that we had taken on our flight in 1931 specifically for Bob was on his desk and had always been on his desk wherever he worked he said.

Unaccustomed to all the adulation, not skilled in the social graces, and completely untutored in public speaking, Russell and I were more than a little uncomfortable. Had we not had the sympathetic and diplomatically oriented Joseph Grew at our side, we would undoubtedly have made a horrible mess of the whole thing. I can't tell you how dependent we were upon him and how grateful for his tactful guidance. We were his dutiful servants, happy to follow his lead. Not until much later did we realize that we had been granted an audience with the Mustapha Kemal Pasha, the president of Turkey, when visiting heads of state were unable to gain even an introduction to him.

Many years later I received a copy of Ambassador Grew's Congressional Record, through Russell's youngest sister, Sandra Grummon, whose husband was connected with the diplomatic corps. For the first time I fully appreciated the impact that our flight had on promoting goodwill between the United States and Turkey and, was a marked advancement in aviation for the world. I wish that Russell could have read Ambassador Grew's glowing

Above: Presentation by the Mustafa Kemal Pasha of the Turkish Aviation Society's highest award. Left: The Turkish Aviation society award—the diamond pin.

account. He would have been as touched as I. According to Grew, Russell was dignified and a completely credible representative of the American people. I was a fox terrier, glib of tongue, hyperactive and appealed to some of the native Turkish populace. All in all, I believe that our feat served our country well.

The next few days in Istanbul were filled with elegant banquets and receptions. We had been outfitted by the Turks with clothing suitable for the activities we had to attend. We had carried only one suit of clothes each on hangers in the back of the *Cape Cod*, so we were wholly dependent upon our hosts to supply all our other needs and they did quickly and well. We were wined, dined, and entertained with dances, swimming parties, tennis matches and moonlight rides on the Bosporus.

Our visit to meet the Mustapha Kemal Pasha was via his private yacht and launch to his retreat in Yalova. Here the Ismet Pasha made a speech and ceremoniously pinned the Turkish Aviation League's highest decorations on our lapels. The star and crescent of Turkey is at the center bottom. Curving upward and inward grace-fully are wings encrusted with diamonds. They are joined at the tips by a platinum star set with a single large diamond. Between the wings is a tiny diamond airplane with a sapphire for the engine in Russell's and with a small emerald in mine. I understand that another such medal was presented to Charles Lindbergh's mother for his flight in 1927. One was also presented to a Russian who flew over the Black Sea. The only others we know about were presented to two Turkish flyers and now are in the museum in Istanbul.

The marked success of our venture made us contemplate again, at least briefly, continuing our conquest to India and Japan. Permission had already been requested and granted by the Department of State on July 16, 1931 to fly to Japan under Embassy Dispatch 138, which stipulated that we would fly to Tachjikawa, Japan. We were not permitted to go to Yokohama and were banned from bringing firearms, ammunition, or cameras. Also, the monsoon season was almost upon us. After examining the *Cape Cod*, we decided that she was as tired as we were. I checked her over carefully making what repairs I could but she had problems. We would fly back to Marseilles and sail for home from there. We were admon-ished by the Turkish official to fly directly over the Mediterranean to Marseilles so that we would not see some of the military installa-tions that they maintained along their vulnerable coastline. We complied in spirit only. The condition of the *Cape Cod* gave is no choice. We flew over the Mediterranean until we were sure that we were out of sight then we followed the "chicken route" along the coastline attempting not to notice the forbidden fortifications.

Our trip to France was without incident. There was a generous crowd of spectators at the airport when we arrived. For shipping purposes, I removed the wings from our weary bird and secured them on either side of the crate I built which was similar to a tent. The fuselage fitted in the base of the crate and was fastened firmly so it could not be damaged. The crane on the *SS Excaliber* lifted our precious cargo from the wharf to the hold of the ship. It was many years, fifty minus a few days in fact, before I knew that pictures had been taken of our prized plane being stowed away in the hold. I

Reception at Yalova with Grew, John, Russell, Mustafa Kemal Pasha and his staff.

now have four pictures taken by Mr. Michael Rotonno, who was communications officers on the particular crossing and whom I met for the first time at the fiftieth anniversary celebration of Floyd Bennett Field, New York on May 23, 1981. It was a great thrill to

The Cape Cod *being lifted into the hold of the* Excalibur *at Marseilles.*

see pictures of the old girl tucked into the freight hold of that vessel so many years ago and to meet the man who was thoughtful enough to give me the photographs in this special year. Mr. Rotonno had heard of the celebration while in the barber chair and decided to make an appearance in hopes of seeing me.

Our trip back on the *SS Excaliber* was a frightening experience. The seas were running high, sixty- to seventy-foot waves for days. The shuddering vessel dove into the trough and climbed the pinnacles of the raging sea as if each crashing wave might be the last that her creaking hull could withstand. I remember vividly the drinking glass in the metal holder in our lavatory. It set deep in the bracket, but the hull vibration was so great that the glass spun incessantly until we finally removed it to a safer place. Most of the passengers were violently ill and remained in their staterooms. The rest of us spent much of our time in the bar talking or playing cards to wile away the hours.

The violent storm in the Atlantic gave way to drenching rains by the time we reached New York. A fireboat had been commissioned to take us onboard well before the *SS Excaliber* docked.

Russell Boardman and John Polando welcomed by acting Mayor McKee,
New York City.

So, amid sirens, foghorns, and the general clamor of the welcoming boats, we were greeted by the hospitable New York officials, our waiting wives, and a throng of well wishers. Customs officials had to be satisfied and they made a big issue of the diamond pins that the Turkish Aviation Society had bestowed upon us, claiming that we owed duty on them. In fact, they dogged our footsteps for a couple of days attempting to assess a fee until the question of our liability for a gift was established. A value of something like $2000 was placed on the pins. I am now told that they are irreplaceable at $20,000 because of the exquisite workmanship as well as the increased value of the diamonds themselves. We were also given beautiful Turkish rugs made by the prisoners and an album of pictures taken by the media at every event we attended in Turkey.

I wish I had a copy of the film of the tickertape parade in New York City. People were hanging out of the windows waving and shouting, throwing confetti and all manner of streamers. Acting Mayor McKee made a brief speech of welcome in the absence of

Russell Boardman, unknown, John Polando, Governor Ely, and Mayor
Michael Curley in Boston, Massachusetts.

Mayor Jimmy Walker, who was away on vacation. There was a banquet and reception before we departed for Boston.

Our arrival at East Boston Airport was a tremendous thrill. Our
families were there and, as always, Boston treats its own with special warmth. The crowd was enthusiastic. Mayor Michael Curley
was at his best on such occasions. He loved the pomp and splendor
of parades. None of the political potential was lost in his handling
of the audience. He was, in truth, a silver tongued orator. We were
so excited that it wasn't until years later as I saw the old newsreel
that I realized that his most glowing, eloquent address was read
verbatim from a written script hidden in a large bouquet of flowers
that he held as he spoke from the podium. I recall with a grin the
reception we attended in South Boston when he stated, unequivo-
cally, "These two intrepid flyers flew over one wave after another
until they saw a vast patch of green and it was Ireland." With that

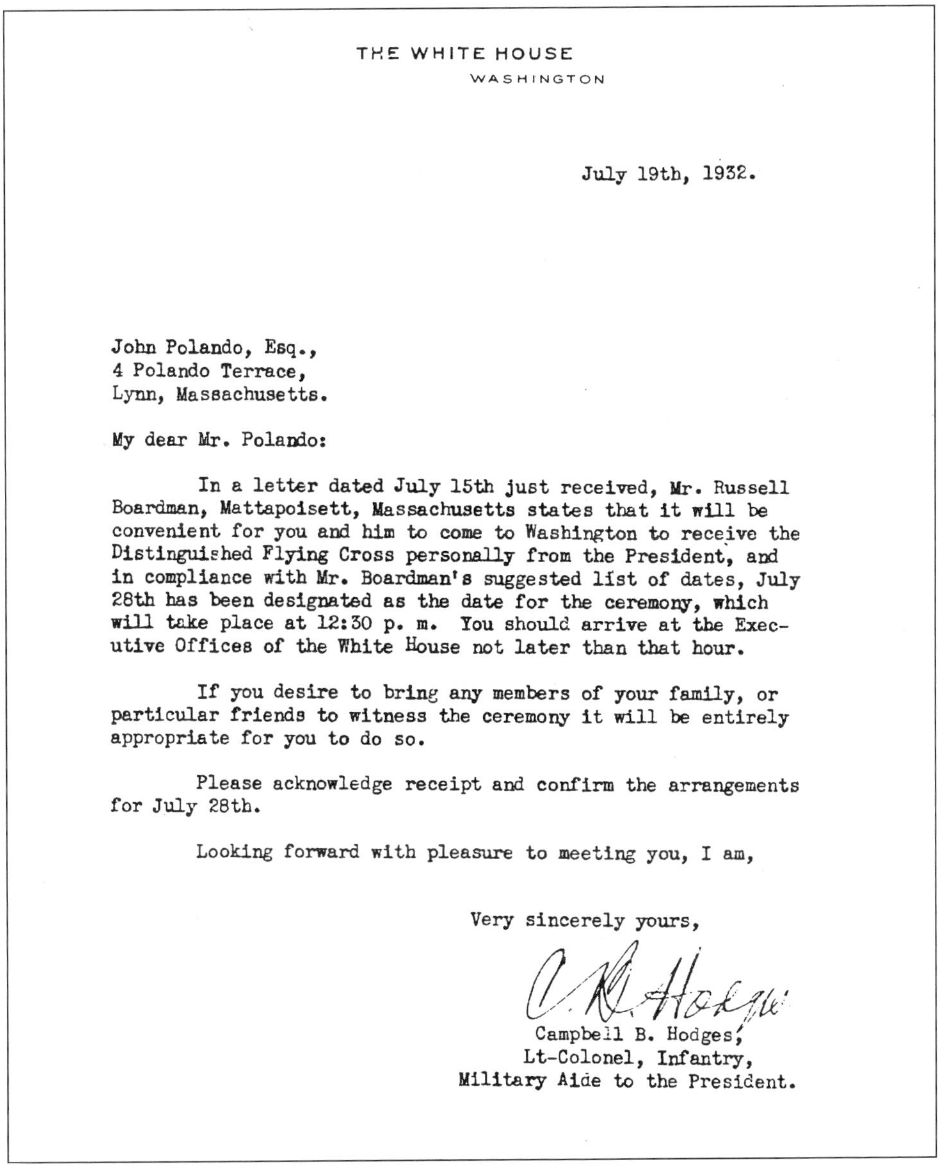

THE WHITE HOUSE
WASHINGTON

July 19th, 1932.

John Polando, Esq.,
4 Polando Terrace,
Lynn, Massachusetts.

My dear Mr. Polando:

In a letter dated July 15th just received, Mr. Russell Boardman, Mattapoisett, Massachusetts states that it will be convenient for you and him to come to Washington to receive the Distinguished Flying Cross personally from the President, and in compliance with Mr. Boardman's suggested list of dates, July 28th has been designated as the date for the ceremony, which will take place at 12:30 p. m. You should arrive at the Executive Offices of the White House not later than that hour.

If you desire to bring any members of your family, or particular friends to witness the ceremony it will be entirely appropriate for you to do so.

Please acknowledge receipt and confirm the arrangements for July 28th.

Looking forward with pleasure to meeting you, I am,

Very sincerely yours,

Campbell B. Hodges,
Lt-Colonel, Infantry,
Military Aide to the President.

Invitation to the White House.

all the "Southy" hats flew into the air and "Honey" Fitzgerald, Ted Kennedy's grandfather, turned to me and said, "He just got a hundred thousand votes on that one."

Celebrations in Boston were followed by an equally warm and friendly parade and dinner party on Cape Cod at The Coffee Shop

Presentation of the Distinguished Flying Cross to Russell Boardman and John Polando by President Herbert Hoover.

in Hyannis. We were presented with handsome large silver trophies and gold cigarette cases with lighters embossed with our profiles and a map of Cape Cod. All those attending the dinner were given similar cases in silver metal carrying a like commendation as a souvenir of the occasion.

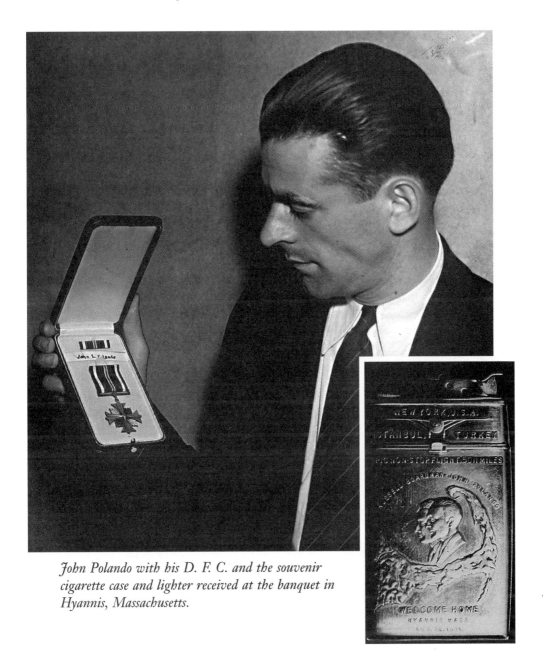

John Polando with his D. F. C. and the souvenir cigarette case and lighter received at the banquet in Hyannis, Massachusetts.

Colonel Edward H. R. Green, of South Dartmouth, Massachusetts, had a party for us and presented our wives with diamond bracelets. Russell and I were given a gold medallion with an inscription and a picture of his sailing vessel *Charles Morgan*. Col. Green had built a sea-

THE UNITED STATES OF AMERICA

TO ALL WHO SHALL SEE THESE PRESENTS, GREETING:
THIS IS TO CERTIFY THAT
THE PRESIDENT OF THE UNITED STATES OF AMERICA
PURSUANT TO ACT OF CONGRESS APPROVED JULY 2, 1926,
HAS AWARDED TO

John L. Polando

THE DISTINGUISHED FLYING CROSS
FOR
EXTRAORDINARY ACHIEVEMENT
WHILE PARTICIPATING IN AN AERIAL FLIGHT

July 28-30, 1931. He achieved a five thousand and eleven and eight tenths miles non-stop trans-Atlantic flight from the United States to Istanbul, Turkey. (Awarded by Pub. Res. No 276, 72d Congress).

GIVEN UNDER MY HAND AT THE CITY OF WASHINGTON
THIS *twenty-seventh* DAY OF *July*, 1932.

RECORDED IN THE OFFICE OF
THE ADJUTANT GENERAL

_____
MAJOR GENERAL

_____
SECRETARY OF WAR

plane base and a landing strip at his property in South Dartmouth. It was the only lighted field on the East Coast at the time. He had been most generous with his hospitality to Russell and me. We would "buzz" the field, the lights would be turned on and by the time we had tied down our plane, Colonel Green's housekeeper, Priscilla Hill, would have coffee piping hot and cake or pie ready for us. Bert Hill was the caretaker for the colonel and a firm friend to all of us who used the field and, I can assure you it was used by a good many aviators.

For the better part of a year, the aura of glamour remained. Russell and I acquired an agent to arrange speaking engagements of us, and he managed to book us in Chicago, Toledo, Cleveland, and many other big cities. We hoped to pay back some of the money that Earl Boardman had invested in our venture. But this was Depression time and cash was scarce. In 1927, when Lindbergh flew to Paris, the purse was $25,000. In 1931 we got

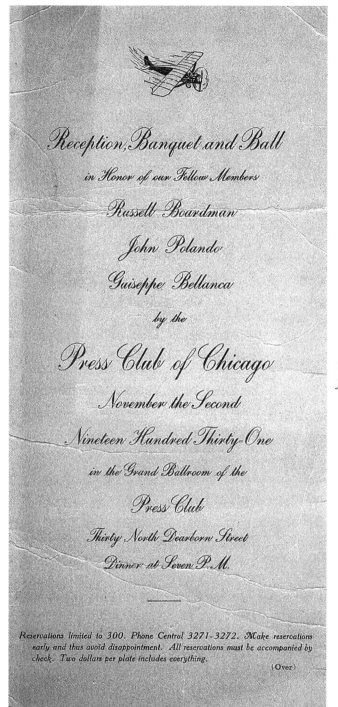

Celebration from the lecture tours following the flight.

Russell Boardman, his wife, Ruth, Col. Green, Miss Mabel Green,
Mildred and John Polando.

$2,500. By the summer of 1932, our speaking fees had dropped to
$100 and our dates were in smaller towns. We still appreciated
being asked, and a hundred dollars was not to be ignored. Besides,
we enjoyed reliving our accomplishment. But, we knew that we
weren't going to get much more mileage out of our 1931 success.

We had also hoped to recoup some of the expenses of our flight
by sponsoring products. We had used Kendall Motor Oil so we
hoped they would ask for our endorsement. No luck. Maybe it was
our lack of know-how or finesse, or perhaps we had chosen the
wrong men as our promoters. Or perhaps it was the times. We did
manage to get into advertising literature for Firestone Tires, which
had served us so well. A baseball card of Russell was made and mar-
keted and lapel buttons were sold in my hometown of Lynn. I
found later that much of the money realized from the sale of the
buttons had found its way into pockets other than mine.

In spite of the speaking engagements and endorsements, and
lots and lots of parties with hundreds of people, we didn't make
enough money to pay for anything more than our day-to-day
expenses. And glamour fades. We had had the heady experience of

TRANSLATION

NATIONAL AERONAUTIC ASSOCIATION

Washington

October 7, 1931

Mr. Paul Tissandier
Federation Aeronautique Internationale
6 rue Galilee, XVIe
Paris, France

Dear Sir:

  We have the honor of sending you herewith the official report of a new record for non-stop airline distance in Class C, established in conformity with the regulations of the Federation Aeronautique Internationale.

  This report has been accepted by the Contest Committee of the National Aeronautic Association and since the performance exceeds the present record for this category, we ask that you homologate the record as follows:

INTERNATIONAL RECORDS

Class C (Airplanes)

  Airline distance – non-stop (United States)
Russell N. Boardman and John Polando, Bellanca monoplane, Wright J-6 300 h.p. engine, from Brooklyn, New York to Istanbul, Turkey, July 28-29-30, 1931 . . . . . 8065.736 km. (5011.8 miles)

  You will find enclosed the sum of 100 francs for entry of the record on the list of international records of the F.A.I.

  This report consists of the reports of the contest officials at the take-off and landing, the photographs of the pilot, mechanic and airplane, report of the Bureau of Standards, barograph chart, report of the U.S.Navy Hydrographic Office, and the correspondence concerning return of the barograph from Turkey to the United States.

  The pilot holds the N.A.A. and F.A.I. licenses. He is of American nationality.

  We regret that there has been some delay in assembling all the reports for this official report.

      Sincerely yours,
      GEORGE W. LEWIS
      Vice-Chairman, Contest Committee

National Aeronautic Association,
Dupont Circle, N. W.,
Washington, D. C.

DIRECTING OFFICIALS REPORT
on
Record Trial
under
F. A. I. Regulations

Record Classification: Duration......... Distance..*III*..Altitude.....Speed.......

Date..July.20,.1931................... Place.Floyd.Bennett.Field,.Bklyn,.N.Y.

Pilot..Russell.Bordman................. F.A.I. No..7004...NAA License No..285...

.... F.A.I. No.........NAA License No........

Crew..John.Polando.....................   ....

Plane.Bellanca................... Mgr..Bellanca..........Type.Monoplane..........

Engine..Wright.J-6............... Mfgr.Wright..........HP.300...................

Course..........................Laps.................Distance................

Course Description.Floyd.Bennett.Field.to.Istanbul,.Turkey...................

...........................Certified by ....

Payload.......................Weighed by ....

Barograph No..23470...............Sealed by..W.D.Ward........................

Remarks: I.certify.that.as.Directing.Official.of.this.record.flight.I...

land-sealed.and.installed.the.Barograph.in.the.plane................

W.J.Hallahan	Walter D. Ward
Official Observer	Directing Official
Daniel Moulton	Walter D. Ward
Official Observer	Official Timer

_____
Official Observer

NOTARY: NOTE: Forward report in triplicate
                              with photos and certified map
W.J.Hallahan   of course.
                   My commission expires 3-30-33

being front-page news for several weeks, but then we drifted to pages two, four, six, and finally out of sight.

I think I should explain a little more fully why Russell and I decided not to extend our flight to Japan as first intended. One of the problems that was ever present on radial engines of the 1920s and 1930s was excessive cylinder head temperature. On occasion the heat would cause a spark plug to pop-out and hang dangling on the connecting wire. Before our departure from Floyd Bennett Field we thought we had found a solution to the problem. A man from Long Island sold us, for one hundred dollars, an alamite gun worked by a plunger in the cockpit. The small tank containing lubricant was mounted on the firewall and little copper tubing was attached to the intake and exhaust ends of the rock arms carrying lubricant to each cylinder. Normally, we lubricated each cylinder by hand after every twelve to fifteen hours in the air. Even after such a brief time we could hear the overhead cylinders squeaking. The cylinders on the bottom were in good shape because the oil tends to flow downward.

We had mounted the device with great care feeling confident that it would be effective on our long journey. Each time we used the plunger we were sure we heard a real improvement in the sound of the engine. Russell remarked that it seemed to purr and I heartily agreed. But, when I checked the *Cape Cod* after we arrived in Istanbul, I discovered that we had plunged all the oil on the underside of the fuselage right down to the tail wheel instead of into the cylinders. The large piece of tubing that fed the smaller ones had broken off at the edge of the cowling.

When I inspected the engine, I took off the rocker box cover and saw that the rocker arms were so badly burned that they would walk off the ball stems, and all the bearings were gone. I took out a push rod and found no ball on the end of the rod. I peened the rocker arms as best I could, greased her by hand, checked the timing, and the valves and ran her up. She turned 1650 on the ground. Obviously, she was more than weary; she was sick and in no condition to continue.

11

Challenges to the Record

•

The establishment of any record is challenged immediately by others eager for accolades. The day after we landed in Turkey, the British revealed that they had a new long-range monoplane manufactured by Fairey Aviation that would be piloted by Squadron Leader O. R. Gaylord and Flight Lieutenant D. L. Bett. They proposed flying a test hop to Egypt. The long distance record would be attempted from, Cromwell, Lincolnshire, to Cape Town, South Africa, a distance of 5990 miles.

By August 27, France had selected four teams to try to recapture the record that we had so recently broken. One of the teams consisted of Captain Bossoutrat and Lieutenant Rossi, who planned to fly from Africa to Madagascar.

The side effects of our feat were beginning to surface, too. Rear Admiral William A. Moffett found in our accomplishment the sinister possibility that an aerial attack from adversaries in Europe might become a threat to America's safety. The prevailing wind had, to this point, made the trip from Europe to the United States difficult. The idea of launching a sea-air offensive was rearing its ugly head as the military read into our flight possibilities that they had once considered too remote to contemplate.

We, however, were still riding high on the crest of our own personal victory. At the National Air Meet in Cleveland on August 28, 1931, we drew first place on the opening program.

By September 11, the Frenchmen, Le Brix, Doret, and Mesmin had departed from LeBourget Field in Paris bound for Tokyo in the *Hyphen II*. The *Question Mark*, piloted by Codos and Robida, took off immediately thereafter but was forced down near Dusseldorf with a fuel leak. The *Hyphen II* was obliged to land with motor trouble at Anizyle Chateau. If either plane had reached a point 160 miles east of Tsitskar, Siberia it would have broken our record.

The maintenance of the *Cape Cod* during the period of our tour was marvelous. There was a complete overhaul on our return to the states and, thereafter, Wright Engine agreed to do a complete check up after each twenty-five hours of flying time.

During our tour Russell was written up in several magazines as some sort of daredevil. I can vouch for his being fearless, but I knew him well and he was not reckless. The trip to Turkey had proven his thorough attention to detail. Luck is wonderful but being lucky is not enough. I am a fatalist, as are most pilots, but that does not mean I get careless. I do my damnedest then hope that Lady Luck is smiling on me.

Speaking of luck, I remember the night that Russell and I were headed back for Teterborough, New Jersey, airport. It was one of the darkest nights I have ever seen, It was so black, so starless, that we couldn't determine our location so we dropped a flare. It was a one-and-a-half minute flare but, for some reason it delayed igniting a fraction of a minute too long. It fell into the Teterborough marsh and within a minute the dry grass of the marsh had leaped into flame. We decided that we had better get lost, for there was nothing we could do but pray that someone on the ground would alert the fire department. We had no radio so we were unable to call them ourselves. So, we headed for North Beach, which is now LaGuardia Airport. The headlines the next morning were "Mysterious Fire Burns Teterborough Marsh, No Injuries Reported." Because there was nothing we could do to rectify the situation, we said nothing at all.

This was only one of the many times that we managed to innocently cause trouble. One time Russell was headed for Fairhaven, Massachusetts, and I was to follow him in another plane. I was trailing along when, suddenly, Russell disappeared into a fog bank. I circled once or twice to see if he would reappear but no luck. He and his plane had vanished. By this time the fog seemed to be settling in for the night. I was now pretty much surrounded by it so I decided to land. The only visible spot was the front lawn of a house in Acushnet, Massachusetts. I almost completely destroyed the garden and lawn in the process. I managed to get a ride and join Russell for the night in Mattapoisett. The next morning we returned to the scene, tendered our apologies for the damage and made arrangement to pay for the repairs to the garden and picked up the aircraft. I knew that Russell knew the area like the palm of his hand so the fog was to him only an inconvenience.

12

County Fairs and Barnstorming

·

In 1932 I was working still, or again, for Wright Engines. Weekends found me carrying passengers as before, making test flights as before, hauling photographers, dropping off parachutists, and doing just about any form of flying that could be crowded into evenings, Saturdays, and Sundays. The fact that I spent five days each week at the airport did not lessen the urge.

I was managing a little Portsmouth, New Hampshire, Airport, which was just off Route 1 and half mile south of the city. We used any aircraft not in use, a Waco, Travel Air, Kinder Bird, Robin, Bellanca, J-5 Stearman, Stinson, Curtiss Wright, or Fairchild, whatever was available. I did a lot of cross-country flying, mostly in New England. In May of 1932 I flew to the Saugus Race track and raced an automobile with a Travel Air. Most of my time, however, was spent in a Kitty Hawk with a Kinder engine, registration NC 33V. There was an eclipse on August 31 that year and a passenger hired me for fifteen minutes to get a closer look at it. We got closer to the eclipse only by some eight hundred feet or so, but who was I to argue? On October 13 I flew for a friend, Frank Huntress, who was the treasurer of the Burrows and Sanborn Department Store in Lynn, Massachusetts. They were celebrating the sixtieth anniversary of the dry good store and wanted advertising flyers tossed out of the airplane. I took a friend along to handle the pamphlets. He did, but not all of them. When we got back on the airstrip, he took great handfuls out of his jacket where he had tucked them to keep warm. I was furious, but he claimed that he nearly froze to death in the open cockpit. Two days later I flew a parachutist in Providence, Rhode Island. That same month I flew for Noyes Buick of Boston for an advertising promotion. There were numerous photo sessions, too, one of them over Cape Cod covering a forest fire and another taking aerial photographs of a golf course in Lynnfield. I would do anything just for the joy of flying.

The year 1933 began in much the same fashion. I did some stunt flying in Fitchburg in an air show in June. That same month I flew to Montpelier, Vermont, with Art Farnsworth in the Curtiss Wright Sedan. I added a few more planes to the growing list in my logbook, an Eaglerock, a Cessna, a Bull Pup, and a Monocoupe with a Wright engine. I can't now recall just how many different airplanes I have enjoyed, but you can bet that each one was an experience that I would not have wanted to miss. Each one was an education and a challenge, and each one was unique. You can't know it all, so you must be open to new ideas. This had been my life-problem and solution, discovery, and application, ever expanding my capabilities. Best of all, I love it.

13

Springfield Aviation, the Gee Bee and Russell's Death

·

Aside from Bellanca, one aircraft company had a far reaching effect on my life and my friendship with Russell Boardman. That company was Springfield Aviation, run by the Granville brothers, developers of the dynamic and, unfortunately, often lethal Gee Bee R1.

The Flying Silo, as she was affectionately known, was revolutionary in almost every respect. She was cylindrical in design, with the cockpit well behind the trailing edge of the wing. The wing area was minimal. She was, by undisputed agreement, overpowered to a dangerous degree. I received a letter dated March 10, 1932 written by Zanford D. "Granny" Granville, one of the five brothers, suggesting that I invest in the development of the Gee Bee. The Thompson Trophy and the Bendix Trophy purses combined were to exceed $20,000 at the Cleveland Air Races, and the Granville brothers were eager to enter both events. The Thompson Trophy was for speed with minimum risk; the Bendix Trophy demanded a little more wing area and gas capacity to carry the ship from Los Angeles to Cleveland, for this award was for distance as well as speed. As fortune would have it, I was in no position to invest. In the end, the Gee Bee did enter the race piloted by Jimmy Doolittle, the only pilot to have mastered its peculiarities, and it won the Thompson Trophy. The little plane, however, was to kill five fine pilots, including my friend Russell Boardman, in its relatively short career. Granny himself died in a fiery crash in 1934.

Russell had been making a test flight in the Gee Bee on August 16, 1932 when she went completely out of control at 800 feet and crashed into tall underbrush. Russell sustained a severe concussion, possible internal injuries, and severe lacerations. His condition was so serious that he was given a fifty-fifty chance of pulling through.

Russell Boardman with the Bee Gee by Granville Brothers. 1933.

The day before the accident, a Monday, he had set an unofficial speed record of 300 miles per hour in the R-1 but the tricky little plane had nearly groundlooped on him.

There has been much speculation as to the cause of the crash of the Gee Bee R-1 that killed Russell on July 6, 1933. It occurred on takeoff in Indianapolis. The plane had a full load of fuel but did not burn, which is a miracle in itself. But it flipped over on takeoff, causing Russell to strike the back of his head with such force that it broke his neck. He never regained consciousness. It was his brother, Earl, who flew to Indianapolis and brought Russell's body back to Cape Cod. He was buried in Westfield, Connecticut, the tiny village where he was born.

SCENES AT BOARDMAN FUNERAL

Russell Boardman's funeral in Westfield, Connecticut, July 1933.

It was a dreadful blow to his family. He left a wife, Ruth, and a small daughter, Jane, his brother, Earl and three sisters, Claire, Alice, and Sandra, who all adored him. It was almost as severe a loss to me as to the family, for he had been closer to me than my own family. He had been my cherished, respected, devoted friend, and my life would never be the same again. My lifestyle as well as my ambitions had been irrevocably influenced by the deep friendship we shared and they still are. I miss him now, fifty years later, almost as much as I missed him in July 1933.

14

Mullison's Scoop

•

After Russell's untimely death I kept myself busy, probably busier than ever before, in an effort to forget the tragic loss of such a fine friend and wonderful man. This did not, of course, work, but keeping occupied helped somewhat.

I managed, in my spare time, to put together a small flying circus that would perform in the New England area. We put on shows and carried passengers for a dollar a head. Our bookings were pretty steady during the summer, for all the county fairs still found that air shows drew a crowd. There were also small air shows in several towns because new airports with a hangar and a grass strip were springing up everywhere. A few fields, such as East Boston Airport, had a surfaced runway. I was frequently asked to perform when a new field had its grand opening. I must have attended almost every dedication in all of New England. I also knew someone at practically every airport in the area, and I still do. It never ceases to amaze people to find that I know someone at each of these facilities. They forget I have been around a long, long time.

On July 23, 1933, I was working as a pilot, an instructor, a mechanic, and Man Friday for the well-known former commissioner of aviation for the Commonwealth of Massachusetts, New England born, Crocker Snow, at Skyways, Inc., at East Boston Airport.

We had learned earlier in the week that Jimmy Mollison and his wife, Amy Johnson Mollison, were planning to fly from England to New York City. They had told the news media that they would have breakfast in London and dinner in New York, a clever and innovative way of saying that they expected the crossing to take less than twenty hours—a feat yet to be accomplished. They were, at that point, tentatively planning to try for a long distance record from New York to Baghdad on their return to Europe. The plane they were flying was named the *Seafarer*, a name I shall never forget.

John Polando 1933.

The plans and charts for the intended trip were aboard the air-craft, as were official papers, first day covers, and the all-important barograph. The Royal Aero Club called Mr. Heinmueller of Longine Wittenaur who would remove the baragraph from the air-craft on its arrival in New York to verify that the Mollisons had taken off from Wales early on the morning of July 23. The bara-graph is an instrument that validates flight statistics.

In anticipation, Ted Husing and a crew of technicians had flown to Boston in a Curtiss Condor with "JIMMY, FOLLOW ME" in huge letters on the side of the fuselage. A loud speaker system had been installed in the plane and, as it flew over East Boston Airport the microphone blared, "GOOD MORNING, BOSTON," to the personnel gathered on the field.

Excitement ran high. There were ten to twelve airplanes, most with press aboard, waiting anxiously for word of the Mollisons. The ASSOCIATED PRESS contacted Crocker Snow and hired a four place Stinson and a pilot to carry their photographer. I was the lucky guy chosen to be the pilot.

The first sighting was over Newfoundland in the mid morning. The Curtiss Condor gathered its large entourage and one after another, the individual planes took off hoping to be the first to spot the *Seafarer* over the United States. I took off in hot pursuit of the Condor sure that it had some leads that the rest of us would not have. I hadn't gotten very far up the coast, perhaps to Portsmouth, New Hampshire, when suddenly the fog and mist completely enveloped the giant Condor. Disconsolately, the photographer and I turned back toward Boston sure that we had missed a golden opportunity.

As I taxied toward our hangar Crocker Snow came running, shouting and waving his arms. "Don't shut down. The Mollisons have been reported over Newburyport," he hollered over the roar of the engine. "Get back up there." Newburyport is about forty-five miles north of Boston so there was no time to waste.

We headed back to the runway and took off. Our normal departure was a left turn but, for some reason, I turned right and out over the harbor, climbed to four or five hundred feet, and headed toward the custom house tower.

Suddenly, the mist parted and we saw the *Seafarer*. I opened the throttle, for she was far faster than we, and we came up on the left side. Jimmy Mollison was sleeping as my delirious photographer snapped pictures. Then I swung around to the right side and waved and smiled at Amy, who looked panic stricken. I'm sure she thought we were too close for comfort for she waved us away frantically. We stayed with them only briefly, then waggled our wings in salute and headed back to Boston Airport.

On our return we learned that we had a scoop. We had the only pictures taken over the United States of the Mollison's in flight. We

The Mollison's Seafarer *over Wellesley, Massachusetts. The* Daily Record American *news scoop. The only picture of the* Seafarer *taken in flight over the United States.*

had had the fantastic luck to outsmart Ted Husing and his crew plus all the other small planes that were trying desperately to find the *Seafarer*. The next pictures taken of her showed her lying crumpled in the marsh near Bridgeport, Connecticut, where she over shot the field in an attempt to land for fuel.

The Boston *Record American* the next morning had our pictures of the Mollisons, with the houses of Wellesley in the background, as they headed on the last leg of their journey to New York, the destination they never made. The headlines read "MOLLISONS HURT IN CRASH." The page 2 caption was "This exclusive photo shows the *Seafarer*, bearing Capt. James A. Mollison and his wife Amy Johnson Mollison, as it passed over Wellesley yesterday. It was made by Staff Photographer Donald Robinson from a *Daily Record* plane piloted by John Polando, trans-Atlantic flyer, and is the first picture in the nation to be published of the Mollison's plane over American soil." The Mollisons recovered and I saw them again when we all participated the MacRobertson Trophy Race in October 1934.

I suggested to the Associated Press that that scoop was worthy of a bonus. "Listen, Polando," they said, "those pictures were great. You got a million dollars worth of publicity out of this scoop." My regular fee was two dollars an hour so I earned four dollars for a two-hour flight. That was it, no more money, just excellent exposure.

It was, in fact, my season for scoops. Shortly after my good fortune with the pictures of the Mollisons, I was flying a Kitty Hawk with a five-cylinder Kinner engine east of Provincetown, Cape Cod, and I had a photographer with me. We were a mile or so east of the cape when we sighted three Savoia Marchettis, SM-55K, heading out to sea. We caught sight of the white, green and red stripes on the rudder and realized that it was part of the flight of Balbo's "good will" tour heading back to Italy after their appearance at the World's Fair in Chicago.

My photographer went wild. He stood up in the front cockpit and gestured that he had removed his safely belt to get a better view of the departing planes. It was a silent plea that I not make any sudden moves or he could easily lose his balance and his life.

We were in luck. Back we flew to Boston with our precious film. We'd made another "first." Headlines again proclaimed our good fortune but the pay remained the same—two dollars an hour and lots of publicity.

15

Maine Air Show

•

On Friday, August 11, my pilots and I were hosted at an aviation ball. It was the eve of an air show in Patten, Maine, that turned out to have interesting consequences.

The flyers listed were well known in the northeast. One of them was Tom Croce who was a real star. He had received national recognition for his exceptional stunt flying in the national air shows. I was well acquainted with all of the flyers but the last name on my list was that of Kermit Hatt. I knew the others far better than Hatt but some ten years later I was to have Colonel Kermit Hatt as my commanding officer in Great Falls, Montana in the Air Transport Command. It is truly a small world.

The flying circus in Augusta, Maine from September 6 through 9, 1933 was to cause me some gray hairs before it disbanded. The weather turned out to be terrible. It poured rain on Friday and Saturday wasn't much better. As a result, the pilots headed for town and a little diversion. In fact, they had a jolly time of it, so jolly they decided to go back to the field and fly over Augusta to stir up some business. The weather was still not good but they managed to take off and fly low over the city. Then they, to a man, flew under the bridge over the river right in the heart of the business district. No sooner had they landed than the police hauled them off to jail. When I got back to the field, completely unaware of the stunt they had pulled, I was furious. By now the weather had cleared and I wanted to carry as many passengers as I could to make up for lost time. There I was with the planes, decent weather, prospective passengers, and no pilots but myself. I flew until dark, still seething at their untimely prank. Finally I bailed them out. They were ordered out of Maine and forbidden to fly in the state again. I was not included in the order, but it certainly put a crimp in my style and a hole in my pocketbook.

THE WORLD FAMOUS
JOHNNIE POLANDO
Famous Trans-Atlantic Flyer
Will Be Present With His Ship At The
PATTEN AIR MEET
AUG. 11th. to 13th.

and will make a personal appearance with a talk on "Aviation" at the Aviation Ball, Friday Evening, Aug. 11th.

TOM CROCE, Veteran Stunt Pilot of Flying Cloud Air Service will give an exhibition of Acrobatic Flying in his Special Stunt Ship.

SEVEN PILOTS from Pan-American Airways and Ames Skyways are entered in the races.

Lieutenant Geo. W. Shaw	Deane Cunningham
"Spud" Holman	"Skid" Young
Gerry Smeed	Percy Billings
"Randy" Mulherin	"Buck" Sherman
Jimmie Colton	Ervin Cummings
Bob Steeves	Kermit Hatt

and many other well known Pilots will be entered in the various events and will all be present at the Aviation Ball.

By far the largest fleet of ships and famous pilots ever seen in Maine.

DOUGLAS MACODRUM, the Flying Reporter will arrive in his ship Friday to cover the Meet for the Boston American.

R. D. HOYT, Dept. of Commerce Inspector will supervise all events.

Continuous Passenger Flying During The Meet
FLY WITH THESE FAMOUS PILOTS

MILLINOCKET PRESS

Relief supplies of food to ice-bound Nantucket and Martha's Vineyard, February 1934. (above right) Pilots Wincapaw, Snow, and Polando.

February 1934 was a bitter month following a biting, cold January. By February 15 Nantucket and Martha's Vineyard were perilously short of fresh foodstuffs. The ship channel was clogged with ice floes that ranged from twelve to fifteen inches thick. The tides caused these huge chunks of ice to jam into impenetrable masses which completely closed the harbors of both islands. The single-screw vessel that made the trip regularly from Cape Cod was only 5440 tons and wholly unsuited to attempt the crossing under such conditions. This cut off the islanders from all their sources of oil, coal, food, and mail. The islands that were so close seemed very far away.

We could not be of any use where fuel was concerned, but the A & P and First National Stores contracted for three pilots, Lieutenant Crocker Snow, Captain Bill Wincapaw, and me to fly in food. The first flight of the relief ships took off in a light snowfall. Crocker and Bill managed to dodge the heart of the flurries, but I had the misfortune to be in it all the way. Finally, I had to swing back over Vineyard Haven on Martha's Vineyard and make a forced landing on Norton's farm at West Tisbury. I was practically frozen, but we managed to remove some of my cargo to lighten the load. The storm abated somewhat so I took off again bound for Nantucket, my original destination. I had to make a second trip to the Norton farm to pick up the portion of the food I had left behind and again go to Nantucket before heading back to Boston. Bill Wincapaw managed to make three flights that day and Crocker

Snow made one. The pilot assigned to relieve Crocker, Lt. Ray Todd, flew an additional load in Crocker's plane. In all, we flew six missions and 12,000 pounds of meat and groceries to the beleaguered island in one day. John Shobe took an accumulation of five days worth of mail and picked up some 500 pounds of mail for delivery to Boston. On Shobe's return to Boston at 6:15 P.M. a Dr. and Mrs. Ray Gilpatrick had chartered the same plane to take them back to their home on Nantucket. In spite of the bitter winds, Bill made one more trip to Nantucket and back. A family on Muskeget had a food drop for Muskeget is twelve miles from the main island. Just a few years ago, Nantucket was again icebound and I was assigned, quite by accident, the charter to fly the newsmen from Channel 4 to Nantucket and Martha's Vineyard. Similar conditions prevailed on the now much more heavily populated pair of islands. This time, instead of food, I was taking television people to record the plight of the stranded islands.

16

YD Convention-Rutland

•

In June 1934 Art Farnsworth and I obtained exclusive rights to carry passengers at the Yankee Division Convention in Rutland, Vermont. It was a terrific break to get an exclusive on such a deal and we were really pleased with the prospect.

I was flying a J-65 Travel Air and Art was flying his own plane. Business was great. The prospective passengers formed long waiting lines. To accommodate so many, Art and I shortened our hops to perhaps ten minutes; one elongated pass around the flying field, then back for the next passenger. Money was tight in 1934 but you would never have known it. When the Yankee Division held a convention they seemed to spend every cent they had and more. The tickets were five dollars and we flew from sun up to sunset every day.

During one of these flights, I was just out of sight of the landing field in a mountainous area when suddenly a portion of an airplane wing dropped from above narrowly missing the Travel Air. It was followed by a section of the fuselage, then a parachute with a scared but uninjured man waving at us enthusiastically. More than a little shaken, and puzzled too, for I had seen no plane anywhere, I was pleased to see the pilot dropping safely into a clearing, and I headed back for the field. I reported the incident immediately then I was besieged with questions about the other plane. I had seen nothing of either plane but was informed that the man I had seen parachuting to safety had been involved in a mid-air collision. The *Rutland Herald* carried this headline the following day: "Two Die As Airplanes Collide At City Airport." The Bellanca, piloted by William H. McMullen, was on an aerial survey photographic mission with photographer R. L. Oakes when he collided with a Douglas observation plane piloted by Captain Herbert Mills of the Connecticut Air National Guard. Mills was the only survivor.

Two Die As Airplanes Collide At City Airport

Last Chapter Of Life's Story Of Ace Of The Air, "100 Per Cent Mac"

Finis was written yesterday to the thrilling story of an aviator's life—an ace of the air whose career would read like a book of romance if compiled in chronological order. When W. H. (Mac) McMullen's life was snuffed out at noon yesterday in a tragic crash at the airport dedication, the country lost an able airman and a chap whom everybody liked and called, "100 per cent Mac."

When McMullen died, another brave man crashed into the beyond with him—R. L. Oakes, an aerial photographer of country-wide experience.

Both men died in harness, the one a pilot of a Bellanca plane, the other with his photographic instruments and paraphernalia equipped for work.

The two were taking photographs for the Aerial Exploration Survey company of New York of the hills and vales that are incorporated in the Vermont national forest and the proposed parkway.

The plane in which the two met death, was the one which McMullen flew over the Andes Mountains of South America for the Shippe-Johnson Expedition for the National Geographic society. It was equipped with aerial mapping equipment as well as regular air camera.

McMullen dated his aviation career back to the World war in which he attained the rank of captain. After the war, he did what most army pilots did, "barn-stormed," and later affiliated with a large plane manufacturing company. He tested and sold planes. One of his assignments was to take a large number of planes to China and start one of the river routes, which have made China air-minded. He later sold a large order of pursuit and attack ships to the Chinese government.

He came back to America and took up with Lieut. James A. Doolittle as sales partner. Their work took them to South America and Europe. It was after this tour that he joined the Shippe-Johnson expedition. He had been doing mapping work since that time.

Wives Hear Dread News From Police

Mrs. McMullen Immediately Notifies Father of Dead Husband; Mrs. Oakes Pal's Into Dead Faint and Is Carried to Hotel.

Two young wives, who kissed their husbands goodby, shortly before they took off from the Glens Falls, N. Y., airport at 10 o'clock yesterday morning, arrived in Rutland at 9.30 o'clock last night to learn that the mangled and lifeless bodies of their men were lying in an undertaking establishment.

The comely young matrons, Mrs. Myra McMullen and Mrs. Helen Oakes, wives of the victims of the plane crash over the Rutland airport yesterday, were informed of the tragedy as they sat in an automobile outside of the Rutland police station.

ONE SAVED BY CHUTE

Bellanca and Douglas Planes Crash Head-on 3000 Feet Above City Field; 2 Occupants of Bellanca Dead.

OTHER ESCAPES

Both Machines Mass of Wreckage; One Photographer's Plane. Other National Guard Machine.

A brooding silence hovered over Rutland airport yesterday just before noon. The sky was clear and the sun was broiling hot, just the weather for a successful show at the airport where dedication exercises were to be held.

The hum of airplanes above attracted the attention of the few persons who were at the landing field.

The hum became a roar and then a rending, ripping crash, high up in the heavens told of a tragedy there.

Two planes had collided—a huge Bellanca cabin monoplane and a Douglas observation biplane.

In another second, the two monsters of the air were hurtling earthward.

They fell like plummets from 3000 feet in the ether.

Two die in Rutland, Vermont, air collision.

I am not an alarmist at heart, but, after the incident in which I had lost two good friends at the fair and now this accident in 1934, I must admit I was delighted when we completed our assignment and headed for home in one piece.

I don't know if I was hungry or just gullible but I would do

American Legion Air Meet with
Clarence Chamberlain in attendance,
September 1934

almost anything that involved flying. I have certificates of appreciation from the Air Mail Service for making a record breaking flight with the mail from Boston to Newburyport in the 1930s. At about the same time I raced pigeons from New York to Boston. The pigeons had a slight advantage over me because they have a built-in radar systems and the fog I encountered didn't faze them at all. Actually, I won, but not by much.

I ran a little airport beside Route 1 in Portsmouth, New Hampshire, and had one family as a regular customer. Alvin T. Fuller's children were at the airport several days a week. They were good kids and I enjoyed having them around. We got along famously. They had gotten permission to fly with me on several occasions and they loved it. As the summer wore on, the children finally prevailed on their parents to go for a ride with me.

The day of the big event was set, and I was invited to lunch with the family before the flight. I didn't have much chance to enjoy the lunch, however, because the kids were impatient to get going and the Fullers asked so many questions about my qualifications, equipment, and recorded flight time. Mrs. Fuller was apprehensive about flying but finally agreed to go. Mr. Fuller declined and suggested he might go some other time.

Off we went to the field. I helped Mrs. Fuller into the front cockpit, fastened her seat belt, adjusted her helmet and goggles then I did my preflight check with special care. Absolutely nothing could be overlooked. At this point I really didn't care if she went or not but the children were jumping up and down shouting, "She's going, she's going." She could hardly back out now so off we went. I took her on a tour of the area and showed her their home from the air. We flew over the nearby beaches and the harbor, making a pass at Rye and Hampton Falls before returning to the field. When she finally climbed out of the cockpit, she shook my hand warmly and thanked me for a "thrilling, exciting experience." For me it was a relief. I had visions of a forced landing, which was not uncommon no matter how careful you were with maintenance.

17

MacRobertson Trophy Race

•

Although I have never spoken enthusiastically of my participation in the MacRobertson Trophy Race of 1934, in retrospect, it was a wonderful experience. It was an opportunity to meet and mingle with the undisputed aces of the aviation world and to travel to cities and countries whose very names were strange and new to me.

The MacRobertson Trophy Race was a celebration honoring the centenary of Melbourne, Australia. The race had two separate categories or classes; the speed competition and the handicap event; which were held concurrently. Our entry, the BABY RUTH, was in the latter class. No race before or since has had such a prestigious list of entries. No sporting event of any kind has surpassed that race for glamour or excitement. None has been more honored by royalty or gathered a more enthusiastic crowd of well wishers. King George V and Queen Mary honored us with a surprise visit on the eve of our departure. The Prince of Wales, who was later to become Edward VIII and eventually the Duke of Windsor, flew in to inspect some of the aircraft and wish us all Godspeed. He was a delightful, dapper, interesting and charming chap, and he took the time to shake the hand of every participant in the race. He even autographed the cowling on the *Baby Ruth*.

There were sixty-four entries from thirteen countries signed up to fly the 11,123 miles from Mildenhall, Suffolk, England to Melbourne. Of this field only twenty were on the starting line at dawn on the morning of October 20, 1934, and we were one of the lucky ones.

Jack Wright had contacted me late in the spring of 1934, with his proposition and what meager details were available at the time. Just how I was singled out I do not now recall but I must presume that my flight with Russell in 1931 and all the interest that that had generated was one factor. The clincher could have been that Lynn

Jack Wright with the monocoupe Baby Ruth.

Chamber of Commerce and all the other service clubs in Lynn were willing to back me financially. The City of Utica was to sponsor Jack Wright. Lynn set a goal of a thousand dollars to help defray my expenses. In return for donations, the citizens were given a certificate of "good will" with my picture on it and on the reverse side a small map of the route we would be taking. In spite of a lot of publicity, the donations were to finally only realize about six hundred dollars.

One thing bothered me, however. It was the lack of organization. Unlike my trip with Russell Boardman, where every detail had been worked over painstakingly by the two of us until a solution was found, the preparations for this race were somewhat sketchy and uncoordinated. The close cooperation that had made a winning

The plane we would fly was a clipped wing Lambert Monocoupe powered with a 145-horse power Warner engine. She was small, trim and dependable and was fitted with a deep cowling to increase our speed. Other than "landing rather like a gliding brick" as one writer put it, she was quite capable of completing the long journey.

Jack Wright and John Polando as participants in the MacRobertson Trophy Race London-Melbourne 1934.

team in 1931 was lacking in 1934. Foolishly, I blamed most of the uncertainties on our not having much time together and assumed that everything had been carefully planned by Jack. After all, it was his plane and his plan. I would undoubtedly, be briefed on the voyage to England and we would be in readiness well before October 20. We were not to learn until later how serious our financial status had been and still was.

On October 5, 1934, after untold complications over accommodations, passports and the safe stowage of the plane on the deck of the SS Olympic, we were finally on our way. Because we had no fittings on the *Baby Ruth* for hoisting, she was secured by the landing gear and by a hawser tied just forward of the tail section then lifted gently aboard.

The sturdy tugs pushed and prodded the great ship out of New York harbor amidst streamers and confetti, the blowing of horns and the general commotion that accompanies departures. We finally retired to our tourist class stateroom to settle in. A pile of luggage occupied the corner of our modest quarters and the dresser had stacks of unopened mail that had been tossed there awaiting a quiet moment.

I emptied my suitcase then tackled the pile of letters. There were the usual messages from wellwishers and friends but there were others too that revealed that Jack Wright did not own the *Baby Ruth*. The letters indicated that Jack owned only a very small percentage of the total investment. The builder owned a portion, the bank owned a piece, and the Utica Civic Association owned a part. My ten percent of the prize money, if we should win, was a joke. We were in hock to someone for almost everything we could raise. In fact, in order to disembark in England with the *Baby Ruth* $420 had to be cabled to us before we docked. Our departure from New York had been financed by a loan from a friend of a friend, the Coca Cola salesman, at the last minute. We were short about $165 before we could leave the ship.

To top it off, Jack developed a weepy case of homesickness and self-recrimination before we were out of sight of land and said he should never have embarked on this venture, but stayed safely home with his wife and children. This was an unpropitious beginning for any endeavor of any kind, but most particularly when our lives were at stake.

The only other American entry sailing on the *SS Olympic* was Jackie Cochran. She was travelling first class so our paths did not cross on the entire voyage. This did nothing to lift the cloud of gloom that prevailed most of the time. Roscoe Turner and Clyde Pangborn, old friends of mine, and the only other American entries in the race, had sailed a week earlier. Bill Bowen, an old-time buddy of mine, and a fine pilot, had "come along for the ride," he claimed. He said he was our business manager, but in truth, we could never have afforded the luxury. He was, however, about the only bright and positive factor on the whole crossing. He kept us in stitches with his antics and remained with us until we took off on October 20 then he returned to the states.

Needless to say, the money required to get ashore was on hand on our arrival at Southampton. After the *Baby Ruth* was lifted ashore she was towed to a small field, Humble, and from there we flew to Mildenhall. Although Mildenhall was not quite completed, we were among the first to be permitted to land. We had made the flight from Humble in just under an hour which caused one self-styled expert to comment that we, should we continue to perform as well, might just win the handicap race.

The days that followed were occupied with briefing sessions, formal and informal parties and more briefing. The International Commission on Aerial Navigation had made the rules and the preparations for the race were thorough in every detail. There was to be no stunt flying, no aircraft permitted without proper precautions and no "hot rodding." Everything was to be strictly by the book. Each pilot had to give evidence of his competency. The number of crewmen was optional but the pilot in command was to remain in that capacity until the completion of the flight to Australia. Wright was to be our P. I. C.

Daylight was just breaking on October 20 when the first plane lifted off at Mildenhall. Jimmy and Amy Mollison had drawn first departure. The crowd was estimated to be in excess of 50,000-an astounding number of people at such an early hour. Jack and I departed at 6:36 A.M. in our assigned slot and headed for Marseilles, far to the south via Lyon, France, where we made a brief stop for fuel. The weather was bad. Above 10,000 feet we would have had to contend with ice. The first leg took us three hours and fifty minutes. From Lyon to Marseilles we saw some improvement in the weather and arrived in Marseilles in one hour and twenty minutes. We were making good time and were pleased with ourselves and our progress.

By the time we departed for Rome, the clouds and mist were well behind us. Skies were a brilliant blue and the next three hours and five minutes passed quickly and without incident. Jack and I shared the flying, so neither of us was particularly weary when we arrived.

I shall never forget Rome. Our reservations had been arranged in advance by the race committee although we paid for our own accommodations. After checking in with the race committee representatives, we headed for our quarters. It was a beautiful and very swanky hotel. My Italian name belied my background for I speak no Italian nor do I understand it. The desk clerk greeted us warmly and carried on at great length while presenting us with our room key. Jack and I nodded our appreciation and were ushered to our room. As the door closed behind the bellhop, we burst out laughing for neither of us had the vaguest idea what had been said.

We relaxed for a few minutes, then proceeded to shower, shave, and don clean shirts and pull on the same trousers and sweaters we had worn all day and head down for dinner. I do not know who was most chagrined, the maitre'd or Jack and I, for the dining room was ultra formal with flowing white table cloths, fresh flowers, gleaming silver, sparkling crystal and it was crowded. Dinner was a nightmare. Jack and I tried to be as inconspicuous as possible but the stares of the guests in dinner jackets and evening gowns were devastating. I hope never to suffer over a meal again as I did that night.

From Rome to Athens the next morning we had a bit of a problem. We were over Avignon about a hundred miles west of Athens when our fuel gauge registered near empty. We spotted a relatively flat field and eased the *Baby Ruth* down without difficulty. In no time the deserted field of grain became filled with staring peasants of all ages. Language was only a momentary problem. One chap in the crowd was a quick study. He understood our sign language, primitive though it was and left in a battered truck. It is a strange feeling to be unable to communicate. I discovered that I was speaking louder than normal in an effort to break the barrier. Somehow, shouting seems to be a natural reaction when, in fact, a few hand motions would accomplish much more. Anyway, the people were friendly, almost too friendly as they attempted to climb on the plane. Jack and I had all we could do to keep them off. Eventually, the battered truck and driver appeared with a few gallons of petrol, enough to get us to Athens. By the time we took off everyone of our cigarettes had been snatched by adults and children alike, we had lost valuable time and we had ruined a grain field with the help of all those curious people. I fear the crop never recovered from the incident.

Avignon to Athens was a breeze. We made it in an hour and ten minutes and the weather was great. We spent the night in Athens and departed on the next leg of our journey the morning of the 22nd.

On this part of the trip I did the flying. I discovered that Jack is terrified of flying over water and our next stop was the island of Cyprus. I am not crazy about flying over large bodies of water either but we could not avoid it if we were to complete the flight to Australia. Anyway, he spent the whole time biting his fingernails and spitting them on the floor of the cockpit. There was nothing left to bite by the time we had covered the 180 miles to Cyprus. We made fair time on that leg also.

After fueling up in Cyprus we pressed on to Alleppo, Syria, where we began to experience the intense heat that was to be our undoing.

We left Alleppo on the morning of October 23 headed for Baghdad. Stretched beneath our Monocoupe as far as the eye could see was desert. We saw few trees, mostly it was just burning sand everywhere. Neither Jack nor I nor the *Baby Ruth* was prepared for the waves of scorching heat that were now our constant companions.

After a flight of four hours and ten minutes, we arrived in Baghdad. By now our engine, with its snug cowling, was just beginning to show signs of overheating. She was laboring a little although I was reluctant to admit that a major problem might be developing. Three hours and thirty-five minutes after we took off from Baghdad we were forced to land in the desert outside of Mohamerah, Persia, with engine trouble. We were soon to learn that we were as unwelcome there then as Americans are now.

In the distance we could just make out some low buildings, so I climbed out of the cockpit and started to go for help. I saw men in the distance and began walking toward them. I remember distinctly the terrible heat that burned the soles of my feet right through my shoes. I hadn't gone very far when I discovered that leaving the plane was a bad decision. We were in an area where trespassing was forbidden. In fact, it was not permissible to even fly over that part of Persia.

The men I saw turned out to be Arabs armed with rifles and rusty bayonets. Their expression was grim to say the least. They "escorted" me to the village. We arrived dusty and parched amidst a throng of curious natives and I was placed in a mud enclosure. There was no roof, no door, just the opening through which I had been encouraged to enter and that was now guarded by one of my captors. We began a strange relationship; I talked to him and he jabbed his rusty bayonet at me. I attempted to get the attention of passersby but they ignored my request even for water. I wasn't particularly frightened of his ancient rifle, it probably wouldn't even fire, but I was deathly afraid of the bayonet. It would give me blood poisoning on contact.

For twenty-four hours I was thus detained. I found out later that Jack fared far better than I. A couple of hours after I was

Baghdad taxi service via jackass and camel.

Routine fuel stop enroute.

ushered into town, he was picked up by some men in an oversand vehicle who were attached to a British oil outpost. On their return to the compound, they contacted the British embassy, then the United States embassy, and the local establishment to resolve the problem that we had caused by landing in the restricted area. While they awaited clearance, Jack was treated royally by his hosts, who were delighted to have a visitor so recently in England. Eventually the matter was settled. I was released, the airlock cleared on the *Baby Ruth* for that had been our problem, and we departed.

Our next stop was Shibia, a Royal Air Force Base some thirty-five minutes away. Here I removed the fuel tank and lowered the standpipe so that it extended less than an inch into the tank. The motion of the fuel over the standpipe had caused the airlock problem for it stood too tall and sucked air instead of petrol.

But our problems were just beginning. The snug fitting cowling and the excessive heat of the desert were rapidly burning the valves. Even the inexperienced ear could detect the hissing sound. There was nothing that could be done at this point. The cowling could not be removed and the blistering heat persisted.

The *Baby Ruth* hissed on to Bushire, to Jask, to Karachi, and Allahabad. Finally, reduced to 100 miles per hour, we brought her down on the dusty Dumdum Airport in Calcutta on October 28. We had made our last stop. Thoroughly tired, discouraged, hot, dirty and broke, Jack and I checked into the Grand Hotel to await money to get us home. Jack made a deal with an Assam tea planter to take him to London and they left Calcutta on November 8 in the hastily repaired *Baby Ruth*.

I remained in Calcutta until I could arrange passage home. In the meantime the British entertained me most cordially. I attended parties in a borrowed, pinned-up tuxedo and nobody even laughed at my dilemma. My memories of Calcutta are mostly of the abject poverty of the Indians in marked contrast to the British living there. The "street people" were everywhere. In the darkness one night I stepped from the curb onto a child sleeping in the gutter. I was taken to the burning burial place of the natives. I saw and was revolted by the filth of the sacred Ganges. It was a moving experience to see how these people existed under terrible conditions. I was practically penniless but compared to these Indians, I was a man of means. The hotel graciously extended credit for cigarettes, food and drinks, hanging small chits of paper recording my purchases on a length of cotton string. I washed my socks and underwear in the bathroom sink each night.

I had first contacted my mother for help and she had declined. I attempted to handle my passage by working my way on a freighter. I was shown the quarters I would occupy and they were not impossible and I would not really have to work my passage but then they showed me the crews quarters below decks. I have never seen such a filthy hole or such a disreputable lot of humanity. The clincher was that the voyage would take seventy-two days.

It was toward the end of November before I finally, in desperation, wired my friend Earl Boardman for passage money home.

I said goodbye to my newly found friends, settled my debts and boarded the Indian Imperial Mail Train on November 22 bound for Bombay where I caught the *Viceroy of India* two days later. We sailed for Marseilles via the Suez Canal, arriving on December 7. I took the train to Paris, where I spent one night, then headed for Cherbourg where I boarded the *SS Bremen* for the last leg of my journey home.

As I look back at the experience, I must say it had its good moments. The British were marvelous to us. The only flaw in our entire stay in England was the friction that was evident between the British and the Irish. The *Irish Swoop*, an American built Bellanca, was Ireland's entry in the race but at the eleventh hour, they were disqualified over total amount of fuel they were permitted to carry. It had involved the difference between the British and the American gallon weight. We all had partaken of their hospitality at the tent they had erected on the field offering tea and sandwiches to us all. Without warning the tent was dismantled and set up across the road on a farm. Most of us felt that the whole thing was rigged to eliminate them from the competition. Everyone liked them with their warm handshakes and ready smiles.

On the trip itself we had been approached in Baghdad by the masseur stationed there to give Jackie Cochran a massage. A colorful tent had been pitched with a large sign reading "Welcome Jackie Cochran." The man in charge asked me, "I beg your pardon, sir, but have you seen Miss Cochran? We've been here for some time now and I don't even know what she looks like." Poor chap, I guess he never did find out, for Miss Cochran's plane had the misfortune to collapse the landing gear early in the race and was unable to continue. Jackie had been listed as the pilot in command although much of the actual flying was done by an old buddy of mine, a former airmail pilot by the name of Wesley Smith. The plane was a Granville monocoupe, *The Hornet*.

Of all the cities where we refueled, only the largest had a surfaced runway. Most were grass fields and, of those Cyprus fueled us from drums, Allahabad supplied us from a fuel truck as did several of the other stops. In Jask we were only the second and third white men ever to set foot there. In Alleppo I was taken to the hotel on camelback, not my favorite type of taxi. Neither the driver nor the beast had good dispositions and neither had bathed in a long, long time. Jack got lucky and drew a jackass.

Of the twenty crews who bravely departed Mildenhall on October 20 only six finally finished the race. C.W.A. Scott and Campbell Black, the British pilots, were the winners of the race logging 11,300 miles in 70 hours 59 and 25 seconds. K.D. Parmentier and J.J. Moll, the Dutch team, came in second in their American built Douglas DC-2 with Wright Cyclone engines. Colonel Roscoe Turner and Clyde Pangborn placed third in their Boeing 247D transport with Pratt & Whitney Wasp engines, arriving only 2 hours and 44 minutes after the Dutchmen.

This story would not be complete if I failed to relate the most recent events. In June 1983 I was contacted by the NOSD Television Aeronautical Staff in the Netherlands. They, in conjunction with KLM, were producing a documentary on the MacRobertson Trophy Race to be released in October 1984, the fiftieth anniversary of the Race. A DC-2 loaned by its owner, Colgate Darden, III of Winston-Salem, North Carolina, was to star. The staff had been able to locate just seven pilots, including me, who had taken part in the Race. Of those seven, I was the last to be interviewed and was informed that I was the only one of us still flying commercially.

My wife and I were invited to Norfolk, Virginia, where my interview took place. We had the great good fortune to see the grand old DC-2, divested of her wings and tail surfaces and ready for shipment to Amsterdam, where she would undergo a complete overhaul in preparation for the recreation of the flight in 1934 of Parmentier and Moll.

On Sunday, August 14, 1983, I flew Lt. Col. Stuart Boardman

Documentary recreating the DC-2, winner for the Dutch team in 1934 for the fiftieth anniversary celebration. The Uiver *dismantled for a complete overhaul. Pictured with John Polando is Colonel Stuart Boardman McCurdy, 1983.*

The Uiver *dismantled and ready to be shipped to Amsterdam for overhaul.*

Reenactment of the MacRobertson Trophy Race in 1984. DC-2 being read-ied for role in the 50th anniversary trip. Photograph by Col. Stuart McCurdy.

The Uvier *ready for her final flight to Melbourne.*

McCurdy's midget Mustang into the Norfolk airport while the team of Ms. Boomkamp, public relations representative, Rob Swanenburg, producer, Hans, cameraman and Aart, soundman, recorded our touchdown. The incoming traffic made recording a conversation impossible so we retired to the pilots lounge. While the camera ground and the producer asked questions I talked about our flight in 1934 remembering more than I thought I could. Perhaps it was just that they asked the right questions. All the while Stuart McCurdy was taping the Dutch crew on his VCR and making his own record of the interview. Stuart's version let me see the interview from a very different prospective when he played it back that evening at home.

Out of all this I had vague hopes of being invited to accompany the crew with the DC 2 to Melbourne in December. Those hopes were dashed when they explained that they had no extra room and that the insurance was dreadfully expensive on such a venture without the extra expense of a passenger.

On December 18, 1983, the great silver *Uiver* departed from Mildenhall with the recording crew and retraced the route, as nearly as is now possible, touching down in Melbourne on

February 5, 1984. They were very good about sending us pictures of the stop in Athens and finally in Melbourne, but I now seem to have lost touch with this able and interesting crew. They did write to say that the trip was without incident. The DC-2 performed beautifully, developing a couple of minor cracks in the cowling on one of the engines and that they had some difficulties with the new radios they had installed for the trip. The old radios were fine.

Much has happened in those fifty odd years since the Great Race and the disturbing memories of that aborted flight have mellowed with age as, I guess, have I. Now I realize that I gained far, far more than I lost. If I was asked again, "Will you go?" my reply would always be "Yes, when do we start. I'm ready."

18

Return from Calcutta

·

On my return from Calcutta in December 1934, I went to work for J. J. Sullivan Liquors. Earl Boardman was one of the primary backers of the wholesale liquor distributorship with James Sullivan. Now indebted to Earl for the eight hundred dollars he had wired me to get me out of the predicament in Calcutta, I was anxious to pay him back. More than that, I really needed the job and selling was right up my alley; I liked dealing with people. I was assigned the North Shore, so I was back in my old neighborhood and among friends. The job had a lot of good points. I could cover my accounts on my own schedule and have time for my first love, flying. I did just that. I flew not only on weekends, as in the past, but whenever I had an opportunity. I often called on my accounts in the evening; they didn't mind and I loved it. My log book is filled with flights at all hours of the day and night to fields mostly in New England.

All this time Millie stood by me in spite of seeing me less and less. I was almost never at home. I was too involved in the pursuit of my own pleasures to give her or little John much of my time. This didn't mean I didn't care; it meant that I fitted them into my too busy schedule when my conscience got the best of me, and only then. John didn't particularly like to fly because he usually got sick. I didn't have much patience with that so took him only when I felt I had to. I did take him and some of his friends flying when he was in summer camp. This I kind of enjoyed because the kids loved it and he got a kick out of showing me off to his friends.

The year 1935 was filled with air shows, dedications of airports, which were springing up everywhere and an ever increasing number of student flyers since money had become less tight. Instruction in those days cost a fraction of what it does today, but it was about the same percentage of a person's wages.

The year 1936 started off with a bang. In March there was a disastrous flood in the Lowell, Lawrence, Nashua, Manchester, and Concord area. I was hired to fly officials and photographers over the stricken area. Then, as now, the most accurate assessment of damage and the greatest aid to rescue could be made from the air. I made quite a few trips in the week following the thaw. After all the excitement of March, things seemed to simmer down. I settled back into the old pattern of instructing, hauling passengers, and tending to my job with J.J. Sullivan. Earl Boardman had an interesting and effective way of stimulating business. He had a large home at Holly Woods in Mattapoisett, Massachusetts. With promotion in mind, he added a great, fireplaced-livingroom and a wing with eight bedrooms and baths to accommodate guests, mostly our better customers. He also had a dock and a yacht, a baseball diamond, and some riding horses. Each of the Sullivan salesmen was able to invite a few guests down for a weekend. In most cases I guess it paid but those who abused the privilege were asked only once. It was a real boon for all the salesmen and we had a ball.

By now my family life, if you could call it that, had deteriorated visibly. Millie and I didn't fight. I have a tendency to walk out on an argument—at least with a wife. Actually, she had grounds for divorce and I had no stomach for contesting it. Eventually, the settlement was made and I moved back into my mother's house along with her and my sister, Alberta. My father had died in 1930, shortly before my flight with Russell, something I have always regretted because I admired my father a great deal and our success would have meant a lot to him.

In my off job hours I was managing the Plum Island Airport, just east of Newburyport. Earl owned a plane and, when it was not in use, I was free to use it for students. If it was spoken for, I flew something else. I wasn't fussy. I flew the Travel Air, Kinner Bird, Stinson, Cub, Waco, or Earl's Curtiss Sedan, whatever was handy and not in use.

Thus went my life until 1942. I won a couple of races, took part in a couple of air meets, logged a few more hours, and generally had a good time.

Earl had a camp on a secluded lake in Maine where we flew in with his seaplane occasionally during the summer months to fish for trout. We used to lash our canoe to the pontoons so we could move from lake to lake depending on which lake had the best fishing at the time. It was a wonderful sport. After World War II the air force had produced so many pilots that those lakes are now about fished out and roads have been roughed in to most of the remote areas that we enjoyed so much.

Earl and I had become very close friends, partly out of respect for each other and partly, I think, for the bond of losing Russell, who was close to both of us. We also shared quarters at Logan Airport where we were officers in the Massachusetts State Guard.

With the United States now involved in World War II we offered out services to the Massachusetts Institute of Technology to fly tests for radar systems. We were both accepted and flew experiments on the new technology for several months beginning on August 15, 1942. Earl was then asked if he would fly a special roster of tests with an English Beaufighter aircraft, which was to be delivered to MIT for that purpose. He accepted without reservation so, for many long nights, he and I sat propped up on our beds at Logan reviewing and committing to memory all the information we could obtain about the aircraft. Her reputation was not particularly good in some respects but she was the craft chosen for the tests and someone had to learn the ropes.

On the day of the test hop, we donned our flight suits and, specs in hand, headed for the Beaufighter. We completed a thorough ground check and I started to climb aboard. "Get the hell out of there," Earl shouted. "If anybody is going to get killed, it'll be me. They can't afford to lose us both." With that, I climbed down and helped him fasten his seat belt and harness. I was really upset for I had planned all along to coach him as he went through the checklist and the problems of becoming acquainted with the plane.

He took off without any apparent problems and I watched as he quickly became a speck in the distance. The wait for his return was one of the hardest, longest waits in my life. When the Beaufighter finally reappeared over the airport, I was ready to shout for joy. The landing was, like everything else Earl did, perfect. The grin on his face was so broad that I couldn't help laughing, but I soon learned that the aircraft was just as tricky, just as temperamental, just as sensitive and touchy as her reputation had indicated. Every flight was a challenge to Earl's skills, and Earl, and only Earl flew her complete program. When the prescribed tests were finally completed it was he who delivered her to Florida. There some cocky pilot made a pass at her and Earl chewed him out royally.

"She's mine until I sign her off. Keep your hands off until the paperwork is completed or I'll break your neck." And he would have too.

It was about this time that Earl started assembling a pack of bear dogs for hunting in Maine and New Hampshire. He had contacted advertisers of bear dogs from all over the country and had acquired a manageable pack. Weekends, when we had no other commitment, we were off to track bear. Earl's telephone rang constantly; the bear were plentiful and their food was scarce so they were molesting farm animals and destroying orchards to the distress of the farmers. We spent as much time as we could tracking, for we both loved the out-of-doors and enjoyed tramping for miles over the roughest mountain terrain. We were both in excellent condition and looked forward to the exercise away from the press of business and our duties at MIT. I felt terrific and so did Earl. We were trim and hard in spite of the huge meals we packed away at the end of a long day in the woods.

19

Air Transport Command

•

In the spring of 1943 Earl Boardman and I finally decided to cast our lot with the Army Air Force. We were obviously too old for the draft. I had had some tempting offers from the navy but nothing had been definitely decided by them or me. Instead of waiting, Earl and I headed for Wilmington, Delaware, hoping against hope that we could pass the rigorous requirements for the air force. We were in our forties and long out of school, both serious counts against us, as we fully realized. Surprisingly enough, we both passed with acceptable grades and the physical was no problem at all. There was one minor flaw in our planning, however, Earl was too old to enlist. So I, at forty-one plus was in by myself. We returned to Boston to await my confirmation and assignment. Earl was really depressed. I think we had both hoped that they would review his enlistment papers and reconsider because Earl and I had flown radar equipment at MIT for several months and we were equally qualified for duty in the air force.

After what seemed a long time. I received a telegram in May 1943 ordering "Captain John L. Polando to report to the commanding officer in Great Falls, Montana for service in the Air Transport Command." I was delighted except that Earl and I would not be together. Earl consoled himself by buying my entire uniform right down to my shorts and socks. He even presented me with my silver captain bars. We parted with a bear hug as I boarded the train for Great Falls.

My only military duty had been with the Air Guard, so I was not prepared for the protocol of the air force. I follow instructions to the best of my understanding so, when I was ordered to report to the commanding officer upon my arrival at Great Falls, that is exactly what I did. I called the base from the pay telephone upon my arrival. In due time a staff car pulled up in front of the rather shabby depot and I threw in my luggage and climbed aboard. The

Captain John L. Polando

driver was indignant if not downright rude. A staff car is never provided to an officer under the rank of major, and I was hardly that. My education was just beginning.

The commanding officer of the 7th Ferry Group, 90th Squadron, 557th AAF Base Unit on my arrival in Great Falls turned out to be Colonel Ponton deArce, my flight instructor in 1927 when I was just learning to fly. He was followed shortly thereafter by Colonel Kermit Hatt, who was one of the stunt pilots in my flying circus in 1933. The last commanding officer during my stay in Great Falls was a young Midwesterner, Colonel Johannson. He was an excellent pilot, a fine officer and a gentleman.

After my briefing and the attendant routine of settling in the bachelor officers quarters, I cooled my heels in the ready room for a couple of weeks. I was reasonably sure that they had forgotten all about me. It was the worst part of my whole tour of duty.

Finally my orders were cut and I was assigned to fly copilot in a B-17F with Lieutenant George "Joe" Grovoug. When asked whether I had flown multiengine planes I had replied, "Yes, in a Ford Tri-Motor" without ever bothering to say that I had not touched the controls of Timkin's plane but had been an observant passenger. They didn't press the point, fortunately for me.

Joe was a young Californian. A good pilot, better than he knew, but very nervous. He wore leather gloves on takeoff and landing and each time he wrung out the sweat when he removed them. He was military trained where I was rated as a service pilot, but we liked each other and got along just fine. The B-17 was a great plane and I found it responsive and easy to handle. Frankly, I loved it. We were meant for each other.

By the time Joe and I had completed our first mission, he signed me off and I was eligible to be assigned as a first pilot. So I switched to the left seat and had my own crew of co-pilot, engineer, and radioman. I could fly five to six hours and drop through the belly hatch feeling as fresh as when I started. I got along famously with my crew. We had a mutual respect of one another but I worked them hard and I was probably cursed roundly for that. I know I earned the title of the "Eager Beaver" and was often called "pop" in deference to my age.

Some of the trips on the Military Air Transport Service were thrilling. Many of the pilots had been service trained, flown the required number of missions in Europe and returned to fly military transports. They were mostly a terrific bunch but there were some war-weary hotshots, too. We had a few rides we were happy to walk away from. One such trip was from Cheyenne, Wyoming, to Great Falls in icing conditions with turbulence so severe that I was sure we'd snap the wings right off. Then there was the time on final approach into Seattle, Washington, when the pilot was lined up with an apron in front of one of the hangars instead of the runway. I had not been comfortable dozing in my seat so had gone up to the cockpit and happened to be standing behind the co-pilot when we were on final approach. I'm damn glad I was. That was one close call.

I flew the B-17F and G series from June 1943 to February 1944 when I was sent to Homestead in Florida for C-54 training. That was a serious mistake. My lack of formal education showed up on my test papers shortly after I entered the program. The flying was duck soup but the schooling was a nightmare. I was returned to Great Falls humbled and mortified by my failure. Fortunately this did not affect my record of service in the B-17 so I was back at the old stand and, slowly, my failure became less embarrassing.

Back on November 28, 1943 I had flown into Denver with a B-17 destined for Kearney, Nebraska, with my co-pilot, Lieutenant Donald Lutes. We landed about seven in the evening, so, after checking into the Shirley Savoy Hotel we dropped into the quiet officers club in the Brown Palace Hotel for a drink before dinner. The place was empty except for one navy officer and three hostesses. Closing time at the club was eight o'clock on Sunday nights, so we barely had time for a drink. We sat near the jukebox and ordered two scotch and sodas. One of the hostesses came over and spoke to us. "Good evening" she said. "I know it is almost closing time but there are two girls here who would be happy to keep you company if you wish." "Thanks, no," I said. "If you want to sit down that's fine but leave them where they are." She was smiling as she sat perched on the edge of one of the chairs at our table. She introduced herself and we did the same. I told her that I was from Boston and Don was from Lincoln, Nebraska. "My father was working for Fairchild Aircraft out of Boston Airport in 1928," she said. I explained that I had been working there myself at the time, so the conversation began. "I remember my father and mother speaking of a Captain Bonnelli. Did you know him?" she asked. I had. After that exchange we felt a bit more comfortable. I asked if she knew a good place nearby to have dinner. She suggested the Italian restaurant Boggio just across the street. I asked her if she would join us because the club was just now closing. At first she said no explaining that hostesses were not supposed to leave with servicemen. Then I guess she thought better of it, or I was more persuasive, for she went with us. She didn't have dinner but she did have a drink with us while we were indulging in another one and deciding what we would have to eat. On the menu I spotted boiled live lobster listed under seafood. It was not a common item in Colorado. I went to the cashier and bought a couple of cigars and headed for the kitchen door. I had spotted the chef with a cigar in his mouth only moments before so, armed with my bribe, I pushed open the door and gave him the cigars. I then inquired about the lobsters. He was most helpful and picked through a half a dozen or more until he found a really lively one for me and one for Don, whom I had convinced that lobster was the best thing on the menu. Twenty minutes or so later, our dinners were served and, after the first couple of bites, Don surrendered his lobster and ate my French fries and salad along with his, while I consumed two boiled lobsters with gusto.

When it was time to leave Don and I flipped a coin to see who would take Dorothy home. I won. If I hadn't I was going to pull rank.

When the taxi stopped in front of Dorothy's apartment building, she invited me in for a nightcap. I was sure I was set for the night. I was even more sure when she handed me the key to her apartment and I followed her in. We had gotten well enough acquainted by now and I knew she lived alone, so I was elated. We had that nightcap and a few kisses but then I was ushered out the door. She said that her uncle lived downstairs, and if I had made it difficult for her, all she had to do was bang on the floor and he would come running. So much for "scoring."

I found my way back to the hotel and the next morning I gave Dorothy a ring and asked her to go to dinner with me that night. Don and I delivered our plane to Kearney, then flew back to Denver. This time I was not going to have any competition. Dorothy and I had dinner alone, then went back to her apartment. I rarely talk about myself but I told her about my failed marriage to

Mildred and about our son John. Then I told her that I was going to come back and ask her to marry me. I don't know what struck me. I'm impulsive but I'm not inclined to commit myself like that. I don't know who was more surprised at my announcement she or I. I'm sure she didn't believe me. I'm not sure I believed it myself.

The night we first met she had told me to call her Dode and I had told her to call me Johnnie. I gave no last name. The second night at dinner I told her that my full name was John Polando and she said nothing to indicate that my name was familiar to her. Obviously, she didn't recognize the name. Finally I told her a little about my trip in 1931 with Russell Boardman. She was good listener but I think a little skeptical. I was glad about that. I don't particularly like people who are nice to me because I made the record books. I didn't know until sometime later that she went to the library to see if I was telling her the truth.

Don's and my next assignment was El Paso, Texas, where we arrived on Tuesday night. We had had a mishap with my luggage. A bottle of rum had broken en route and soaked practically everything I owned so my first and most pressing obligation was to hang my fragrant clothing up to dry. Then I sat down and wrote Dode a note. Writing letters is also uncommon for me.

While in El Paso we went to Mexico to do a bit of shopping and I bought Dode three pair of silk stockings and a small replica of my air force wings in silver. I had no idea when I would get back to Denver for our next destination was Long Beach, California.

When we landed in Long Beach I was happy to learn that the commanding officer of the base was an old friend, Bob Love, from New England. He and I had a drink and I explained that I was in a hurry to get back to Denver to see a girl. The best assignment he would give me was a delivery to Salt Lake City, Utah, but, fortunately for me, the weather there was bad and I used Denver as my alternate. Dode and I had met on Sunday and here I had been able to return one week later. I still didn't pop the question, but I did give Dode the wings and the stockings and a promise to return.

Trips to Denver became scarcer than hen's teeth. Heading home on December 18 for a brief leave, I made a stop in Denver. Dode and I had lunch and went shopping for a friendship ring. We found nothing but she had been reluctant to accept such a gift, so I guess it was just as well. After our lunch, I went back to Stapleton

Airport and boarded a flight for home while she climbed aboard a train and headed for San Francisco to spend Christmas with her brother, who was stationed there with the Coast Guard.

I spent my leave with my family and friends and, quite frankly, tried to push this new relationship out of my mind. I didn't work. I didn't write Dode or try to telephone or even wire until December 31. Then I sent a Western Union saying I would be in Denver on New Year's Day.

I arrived at Dode's apartment at about eleven in the morning. She was glowing and full of questions about my trip. I was really happy to be back, We sat in her wing chair, she on my lap, and finally I asked her to marry me. I told her I loved her very much and she said she loved me too. Then she took me downstairs to meet her "uncle" and "aunt," Eddie and Clara Greene. Aunt Clara insisted we have a cocktail and asked Dode to help her. I didn't know until later that I had passed inspection as far as they were concerned.

After that I saw Dode briefly in Cheyenne, Wyoming, when I called to say I had a few hours to kill so she took the bus up, arriving about ten o'clock in the evening. The military were provided rooms so Dode used mine after I left at two in the morning on M.A.T.S going to my next assignment. She flew home the following morning in time to go to work. We didn't have much time together but it was better than nothing. Aside from that, we kept in touch at any and all hours of the night whenever I could get to a telephone. I finally told her that we had better set the date because I couldn't afford the telephone bills.

We did set a date and she gave her notice at the Milwaukee Railroad where she worked to terminate on March 26, 1944.

She was to fly to Great Falls but the small airline was 50 percent out of business. They had one twin engine plane and one engine was in the shop for repairs. All the while the reservations were piling up and civilians were the last to be contacted when they finally were back on schedule so an alternate plan had to be made. The railroad advised her that it was a 36-hour trip and departures were late in the day. The buses left Denver for Great Falls at one in the afternoon and would have her in Great Falls by four the following day, so that was her best choice. Actually, I had planned a party so she could meet some of my friends and the party went on but the guest of honor was not there.

Dode arrived at four Sunday afternoon but I wasn't there to meet her. I had returned to the base at about 3 A.M. and inquired if I had any messages. The sleepy clerk said that no one had called so I arranged a wake-up call in plenty of time to meet the bus. But the clerk forgot to waken me. By the time I got up, borrowed a car and raced from Gore Field to the off-limits hotel where the bus stop was located, I was more than an hour late and Dode looked kind of scared. I had a day's growth of beard for I hadn't taken time to shave. I'm sure she was having second thoughts about having given up a good job, sublet her apartment, and come in a blinding snowstorm to a little hick town to meet a man she hardly knew. On top of all that, she had sat in a smelly bus for thirty hours and then found that the bus company had lost her luggage. After almost forty-two years she remembers it well, but she isn't sorry or scared or lonely anymore.

The air force has a perverse sense of humor, I guess, for they gave me Saturday, April 1 and Sunday April 2 for our wedding and honeymoon. We had a reception at our tiny house and much of the food was provided by the officers club kitchen including a beautiful two-tier wedding cake. The rest we did ourselves. Captain and Mrs. Bill Stenson stood up for us and Dode was given away by Captain Steve Keefe. We have lost contact with the Stensons but hear from General Keefe who lives in New England.

On the Monday following the wedding, I was off on a two-week trip, then home for a couple of days, then away again. On one such trip I was home less than six hours before getting new orders, but we managed. Dode had grown up in a family where aviation was held in high regard, and she seemed to understand that this was not just a job to me but a way of life, and she accepted it as such.

The Air Transport Command was a haven for war weary pilots, and we got our share. Never having been in combat I didn't know how they felt. The let-down must have been tough but some of their antics made the rest of us look bad. They would take a staff car and be gone for a week, or stay in off-limit hotels and rooming houses, and be tossed out of bars. But, for the most part the men at Gore Field were well liked. Great Falls was a small town and there were a great many more military than civilians there in 1944. The town of 1300 persons had become, overnight, a small city of 13,000 which must have been very difficult for the regular residents.

Housing was a real problem for the married officers and their families. Our commanding officer was living over a garage and there wasn't an empty house in the whole area.

I had heard of a Mrs. Sullivan, who owned a small house on Second Street south, and had rented it several times to officers. Unfortunately, at least two of them had failed to pay the balance on the rent owed her when they were transferred so she was reluctant to rent again to service people. Mrs. Sullivan was employed by a jeweler in Great Falls, so I made a visit to make a purchase and see if I could change her mind about the house. I made a purchase and then offered to make a deposit of $500, which would be hers if I should default in my payments. I won. We got the tidy, four-room house and garage and lived happily there for a bit over a year until I was transferred to Cincinnati, Ohio, April 2, 1945.

It was during our stay in Great Falls that Turkey became an ally. When I learned of this I decided that I would add the Turkish Medal of Honor ribbon to the D.F.C. ribbon already on my blouse. The medal itself was suspended from a red and white grosgrain ribbon so I had Dode make up the ribbon for me. I would have had to get copies of my citation, which were in Lynn somewhere, in order to have a ribbon officially made for me. I was entitled to wear it.

The first trip I made after donning my new ribbon took me to Wichita, Kansas. There I went to the officers' club for a drink and dinner and almost ended up in a brawl.

"What in hell is that thing?" some captain asked loudly. I obligingly told him. You would have thought I had called him a dirty name. He certainly called me some unmentionable ones.

Then a colonel came to my rescue, appearing as if out of nowhere. "Cool it, captain," he said. "The Turks have become our allies and this man is entitled to wear any ribbon he has earned." The captain sputtered and turned back to the bar. Then the colonel took me to one side where I thanked him for stepping in but told him I thought I could have handled it on my own. He looked back at the captain, who was not paying any attention to us, then turned back to me.

"Captain, by the way, what is that ribbon for anyway?" I explained and shook his hand as he went back to his table. That was the only time the ribbon was challenged but it wasn't the only time it was mentioned for, to my knowledge, there was never another like it.

About the end of May I was told that if I wanted to make major I would have to "fly a desk" for a while. I was then assigned a job that required a lot of paperwork, something I hate and something I do badly. I would manage to sign the papers that my secretary put on my desk then, I went flying. Consequently, whenever my superiors were looking the other way, I would slip out, take an AT-6 or whatever I could find idle and leave. Most often it was to Glacier National Park, where, if two of us could arrange it, we would do a little dogfighting. If no one else was around, I would chase the elk which were abundant in the area. Once I buzzed the log cabin of the forest ranger and discovered too late that I had spooked his horse. On my next pass over the house I saw the ranger shaking a good-sized piece of firewood at me and my noisy AT-6. I figured that he had had plenty of time to get the tail numbers and call them in to Gore Field, and that my hide would be tacked to the walls when I got back. For several days I waited for the bomb to drop, but it never did. I was lucky again.

In early August 1944, orders were cut for me to fly the hump. This was an overseas assignment based in India where Japan was struck from the land bases on her west. I got the news on Tuesday and was due to leave Great Falls on Sunday at seven o'clock in the evening. We had been fortunate to have a house by ourselves in this overcrowded town and I had promised a major that he could have the house when we left. Dode had packed all week and made her reservations to return to Denver just before I left for Utah to get the training needed for my new assignment. We were upset but there was little we could do about it.

About four-thirty on Sunday afternoon the telephone rang. It seemed that someone had reviewed by orders and found me over-age for such a mission. The problem then was to find someone on Sunday afternoon to send in my place. He had finally succeeded but the major still wanted my house, so I had to talk fast to get him off my back. The plane ticket was easy to cancel so Dode and I went to the officers' club to celebrate.

With the cancellation of my orders for India, I was a displaced person, so to speak, and they had to do something with me. My assignment late in December was for B-29 school in Birmingham, Alabama. We had a leave due in October then I continued to fly B-17s out of Great Falls until my temporary transfer to Birmingham became effective. Dode went to Denver to visit the Greenes for a part of the time I was to be away.

My assignment to B-29 school was great. It was a terrific plane, and I enjoyed every minute in it. Although some models had difficulty starting, my only problem was once when I had a two-star general onboard. As we were making an approach the landing gear light indicated a malfunction. We burned off as much fuel as we could, hand cranked the gear, then finally landed very gently after all else had failed to assure us that the gear was down and locked. It turned out to be a faulty light on the instrument panel.

My duty in Alabama was in checking out pilots in the B-29. I couldn't have asked for a more satisfying job. On one such trip with Captain Paull we landed in Denver and I had a chance to see Dode for the first time in several weeks. The next morning we took a taxi to Stapleton Field, and I requested permission to make a tight turn around the flagpole. Permission was granted. Dode was standing at the base of the pole, tears streaming down her cheeks. I'm sure that request had nothing to do with the fact that the flagpole is no longer there.

Aside from the fact that I had seen Dode only once during my assignment, and she was pregnant, I was sorry to leave Birmingham. That was a wonderful plane.

Our first anniversary found Dode packing again. This time we were being transferred to Lunken Field, headquarters of the Air Transport Command, in Cincinnati, Ohio. We left Great Falls on April 2 by train for our new post. Major Ernest W. Burton, with whom I had served in Great Falls, had been made commanding officer at Lunken and had fought tooth and nail to get me down there as his engineering officer. My qualifications were not quite up to the requirements so he had pulled some strings to get me reassigned to him in that capacity. I did my level best to justify his faith in me, and I think I succeeded.

Only once did I put Major Burton in jeopardy. One of our planes had a forced landing in a corn field in Kentucky. It was a mechanical problem but the pilot was able to land safely and return to Lunken. I took a driver, enough fuel and a few tools, and headed for Kentucky. It never occurred to me to consult anyone. I was going to do something I would rather do myself than ask anyone else to do because it was risky at best.

I checked the plane over, made a couple of adjustments, gassed her up, and managed to take off and get her back home. Then the sparks began to fly. I had been asked by the tower to make a low pass so they could determine what was streaming from my landing gear. It was cornstalks and they didn't even come off on landing and had to be removed by hand. If the corn stalks had not been discovered, probably I would have gotten away with it but I had flown a military aircraft in which I had never been checked out. That is strictly against the regulations, and the punishment is severe. The fact that I had little choice did not seem to matter. Major Burton took a lot of flak on that one but he avoided the disciplinary action that was to have been entered on my service record.

In September 1945 I was mustered out of A.T.C. still wearing my captains bars and not until January 1947 did I receive my majors leaves.

The more I think back on my duty with the Air Transport Command the more I recognize it as about the best two and a half years I have ever spent. I had the distinct privilege to fly some important people in wonderful airplanes and I did it with pride.

One particular night when I was officer of the day at Lunken, a plane landed and an officer came to me to ask for a staff car and driver to take him to a meeting at headquarters in Cincinnati. He said it was urgent and he was running late. I had no driver for the staff car so I decided to take him to town myself. I was aware that I was not supposed to delegate a substitute for myself but there seemed to be no alternative.

I introduced myself and he told me his name was Paul Tibbetts. On the relatively brief ride to the hotel we talked of the usual things; weather, war, stateside duty, then, suddenly he said, "Captain, I have been chosen for a very important mission and I'd like to tell you about it but I can't. You'll read about it in the newspapers anyway." He was right. I read about it and so did the whole world. He was General Tibbetts who bombed Tokyo.

At forty-four I was too old to remain in the service in any capacity except at a desk job. I had accumulated thirteen years of service including the National Guard, the State Guard and the Air Force but there did not seem to be any way I could finish the seven years for a pension, so I gave up. Earl had sold the liquor business in 1943. All that remained was a package store in Swampscott, Massachusetts, which was under agreement to someone else.

Dode, baby JoAnne, and I had no place to go. My mother had no room for us. My brother, Leo and his wife, Judy, took us in and put their little boy in their bedroom so we could have his room. That was kind but rather uncomfortable, so, when Earl invited me and my family to Cape Cod I readily accepted. He was cutting timber and had set up a lumber mill on his property at Holly Woods in Mattapoisett and said he could use me. We remained for about three months but I was afraid we would wear out our welcome. We had one baby and Earl and his Dorothy had two very small children. It was too much to expect them to keep us longer so we left for Lynn.

For the next four months we kicked around from my older sister, Violet's house to a house with friends where we remained until the end of May when we finally found an apartment. We had bought a two-family house and cottage in Lynn but were unable to get the tenants out. The laws were strict on that score, so we waited from April until August for the tenants to move.

I had gotten a job with Pappas Distributors and, weather permitting, I would instruct at Beverly Airport nights and weekends. Here I became acquainted with Dave Emerson and Sandy Loughlin, both fine pilots and genuinely nice people. We had lots of good times together.

In August 1947 Earl asked me to repossess the package store in Swampscott. The lease would expire on August 12 and he wanted me to go in as manager. I knew Eddie Mylotte, who had been running the store for several years and was suspected of being less than totally honest. There was no love lost between us but that didn't make it any easier to go in with a court order and put him out physically. Earl had his own reasons for asking me to do it, and I wasn't about to disappoint him. I did as I was told, and for the next nineteen years I managed Shore Line Import Company. In 1965 I bought the business, the building that housed it and two other stores plus two apartments on the second floor.

During these years I flew some, but not a lot, mostly out of Beverly Airport. In 1957 I had Brownell Boatworks in Mattapoisett build me a 32-foot sportfisherman with a tuna tower and a pulpit. Boating, like flying, is a fair-weather sport so, for much of the summer I spent most of my spare time on the boat. I put in the required number of hours to retain my private pilot's license but not a lot more. One ritual I never forgot, however, was a flight at daybreak each year on July 28, weather permitting, when I dropped flowers at sea in memory of Russell Boardman. The trip to Istanbul with Russell was the high point in my career and in my life. There is something I cannot describe about the experience Russell and I shared; something that touches me deeply to this day. My greatest sorrow is that he was not around to share my small triumphs, little successes, and some failures because I have always felt that he had a hand in all the good things that have happened to me.

In 1969 I sold the package store and the building for the long hours and diminishing returns didn't warrant keeping it. Dode had been working with me since 1964 and she continued working for the new owner for several months until he cut her hours so drastically that she quit and went to work for the ITT Lamp Division in Lynn. I couldn't remain idle, so I drove a courtesy car for Beacon Chevrolet. By now, John Jr., who had played only a small role in my life because he had remained with his mother, was in San Francisco and on his own. Our Joanne had married, and a year later our son Jim had taken a bride, so only David remained at home, and he was due to graduate from high school in 1972. I began to get itchy with not enough to do and I couldn't afford to fly, so we talked about retiring. We really didn't need a seven-room house for the three of us, but, decided to hold off until David's graduation.

20

Retirement

·

In June 1972 a whole new chapter of my life was begun. We had finally made the move to a smaller home in East Sandwich on Cape Cod. Dode was taking care of the yard and doing the painting, so I started hanging around the Barnstable Municipal Airport in Hyannis. I did a little flying at Discover Flying and made myself available. Al Howe, who owned the business, needed an extra pilot on occasion and I was ready. With very little pushing, I got back my limited commercial rating and started doing some of the sightseeing flights for the company. They were easy for me because I knew the territory. I had been flying in and out of Hyannis since 1928, when the airport was a grass field and had one lone hangar.

My working for Al got me acquainted with a host of other pilots, both commercial and private, with a lot of student pilots, although I no longer teach, and with the ground personnel at the airport. Most of them are still around and Dode and I have formed close friendships with many of them. I have flown countless hours in Gene St.Jean's Cherokee 89R, which is a six-passenger plane which now has been bought by another friend, David Sherman. I am free to use Senator Allan Jones' plane whenever he isn't using it. A number of other planes have been put at my disposal over the several years I have been at the airport. There are too many to name and I fear I would forget someone and his feelings would be hurt. I loved being back in the atmosphere that I enjoyed most whether it was out in the hangar with the mechanics or at the coffee machine exchanging stories and experiences with friends. I had a few more hours of flying under my belt than any of the others, and I didn't mind sharing some of the good times, and the bad ones, with this younger crowd. We spoke the same language.

One of the best times we had was when Al Howe bought a Stearman early in the spring of 1973. He and I outfitted ourselves in borrowed motorcycle coveralls for the flight back to Hyannis from New Jersey where he had made the purchase. We wore helmets, goggles, and mittens, but even then we nearly froze to death. I was riding in the front cockpit and had just about all the frigid blast of air I could stand, so I slid down as far as I could in the open cockpit to get warm. I almost scared Al out of his wits. He was frantic when he looked and I had disappeared completely from view. I hadn't been in an open cockpit for so long that I had forgotten the fabulous feeling of flying with the wind in my face although I could have picked a better season to experience the thrill. I managed to do just that off and on for several months. Al was using the Stearman to tow banners, and I was one of the several pilots who did the towing.

One time in particular I had the towing job and had a problem. If you are not familiar with the towing procedure, the sign is laid on the grass next to the runway and the towing cable is secured to a line stretched between two poles, similar to goalposts but much more flexible. The pilot checks with the tower operator to obtain permission to make a low pass to snag the banner. This is done with a tow cable and hook trailed by the aircraft. With any kind of skill and good fortune, the pilot can pick up the banner on the first pass. At least I was usually able to do it.

One day after I had flown the prescribed time, about an hour if I remember, I requested permission from the tower to make a pass over the field and drop the banner. The tower replied, "John, make another go-around. The banner looks odd." So, go around I did and made another pass by the tower. "John, you've got it tangled on the landing gear somehow," the tower informed me. This was not good news, so I asked them to hold any traffic in the pattern until I was able to land.

From the cockpit I was unable to tell that I had a bad tow and I had no idea what I was going to do to get the Stearman down without damaging anything. I decided to make as slow an approach as I could and let the plane settle on the runway. The wheels touched and the tailskid dropped to the tarmac neatly cutting the tow cable and leaving the banner safely on the runway as I rolled to a stop. Everyone rushed out to congratulate me for a job well done in getting the banner loose. Who was I to tell them it was a fluke. I could never have predicted that the tailskid would sever the cable. Lady luck was still riding with me I guess.

When Al Howe folded, I found a home with Hyannis Aviation. That company too under went some drastic changes but all for the better. My boss was Bruce Hoglander, whom I liked and respected very much. He was a bright, ambitious and talented young man.

One of the jobs I enjoyed the most was flying photographers. I had a chosen few and we worked well together. Gordon Caldwell would tell me on takeoff what he hoped to shoot then, laughingly advise me "not to get the wheels wet" with my low passes. I flew Dick Kelsey, Walt Fleming and several other well known photographers on the cape. The trick was to put them at the best possible angle, at the best altitude, and then position the plane so that no strut or shadow appeared in their finished product.

As the years roll by the everyday living of yesteryear has become, in the eyes of some at any rate, legendary. The conquests we made are now a bit of history although we had no idea at the time that we would have any particular impact. I assure you we did it because it was there to do. We did it for glory too, to be sure, but glory is so often short-lived. At least we thought it might be. Our appeal to the general public as speakers and men with a record lasted a little over a year as I said before. We were not hurt or upset. We accepted the fact that headlines would fade into page 30 blurbs. That is just the way it is—or so we thought.

In the past few years I have been asked to speak to several groups of Rotarians, Kiwanians, Lions, Glider Pilot Association, Cub Scouts, Civil Air Patrol members, the Order of Daedalians and others and they still find our accomplishment worthy of note. It is gratifying. It is wonderful to talk of the good old days and to compare them with the astonishing advances we now accept as routine. I consider myself very fortunate and thank God for permitting me to be a part of this modern age. Those of us who lived the legend are few and their numbers become smaller each year. Oh, that I could gather them together and record some of the wonderful feats of the 1920s and1930s. We shall live to regret those omissions I fear.

In 1980, a good and faithful friend, Sam Sirkis, started assembling a committee to honor the Boardman-Polando flight in 1931, on it's fiftieth anniversary. A huge banquet would be held on Saturday, July 25,1981. Sam secured Gene Cernan, the astronaut, as the principal speaker and F. Lee Bailey as the master of ceremonies. The planning lasted for nine months and the program escalated as the ideas became realities.

The year 1981 was to hold additional surprises and honors for the team of Boardman-Polando, and the first event was in May.

Dode and I were invited to help Floyd Bennett Field celebrate its fiftieth anniversary on May 23, 1981. We boarded Provincetown Boston Airlines in Hyannis and flew to LaGuardia for the affair where we were met by a handsome National Park Service officer with his Smokey the Bear hat then taken directly to the field for a buffet lunch.

The luncheon was held in a modest building that literally overflowed with celebrities from the early days of aviation. No program had been prepared for the event for the park service was, I am sure, not aware of the potential with such a group of people. Many had come from as far away as California and Florida to take part only to find that no formal schedule had been established. After lunch the we were all escorted to a grandstand where we sat watching a program of model flying and kite aerobatics and listened to two or three speakers. Half a dozen of the guests were introduced but, when the speakers were done, we were escorted back to our various hotels. The following day there were a few talks and slide shows in some of the conference rooms in the old terminal building.

I was fortunate enough at the luncheon to find some wonderful new friends, so I was reasonably content. A tall, gaunt gentleman by the name of "Slim" Henniker introduced himself to Dode and told her that he was Rev. Belvin Maynard's mechanic before I was. He had a photocopy of a flyer from an event for the benefit of the widow of Reverend Maynard and his four children. The air show had been held on November 19, 1922 in New York and I knew nothing of it because I was just a mechanic in New England.

It was here too, at the luncheon that Mr. Michael Rotonno, who had taken the picture of the *Cape Cod* being lowered into the hold of the *SS EXCALIBER* in 1931,presented me with those great pictures.

Jimmy Mattern had been selected to be one of the few speakers at the Sunday session. Dode attended and reported that, unfortunately, this very talented pilot showed mostly the misfortunes in his flying career not his success and they were many.

I had time before the grandstand filled to walk on the runway that Russell and I had used on our takeoff so long ago. Now it was cracked and grass grows tall in those crevasses. The hangar we used still stood, securely locked, with more windowpanes broken than whole, and badly in need of a coat of paint. In 1931 there were no doors because the building was so new. I could have wept seeing the once proud airport reduced to this. The administration building, which had been closed since the navy moved off the field in the 1950s, had been partially restored to it's original splendor. It housed a famous mural. It was a handsome building in the thirties version of Greek Revival style with tall columns and huge main lobby with a vaulted ceiling. It was testimony to an elegance long gone.

As I look back on the weekend, it was pleasant enough and I had an opportunity to see Teddy Kenyon and Viola Gentry, two unusually fine women pilots who have set their own records in the history of aviation.

Following the affair at Floyd Bennett Field, I was advised by the Aero Club of New England that the Cabot Award was to be presented to me in June in recognition of the Boardman-Polando flight in 1931. Our names follow those of many illustrious persons whom I know and respect. I consider it a great honor to have our names in the company of such greats as Igor Sikorsky and Jimmy Doolittle and all the others. I only wish that Russell had been beside me for it was really he, not I, who made it all happen.

The banquet set for July 25 was yet to come and it had already been a banner year. Little did I know what was in store for me, however, when Sam's committee set their goals. Dode was the secretary but she didn't talk much about the plans. They were to be for me to fly from Floyd Bennett Field, no longer an airport for fixed wing aircraft because of its proximity to Kennedy Airport, to Hyannis. Those plans were handled by Arnie Stymest, Massachusetts commissioner of aviation, who got permission at four in the afternoon of July 24 for the flight.

A Stinson had been obtained from Robert Sprague, who would also provide his pilot to accompany me. There was room for one more person, so Major Clark Boardman McCurdy, Russell Boardman's nephew and a crack F-111 pilot at Pease Air Force Base, went with us, representing his uncle on the flight. The plane was a beauty and all original, having been owned by the same person since it was purchased new in 1931.

We had a great flight up from Floyd Bennett Field after a picture-taking session on the old runway. Our arrival in Hyannis was a heartwarming welcome from several hundred spectators and our families. Cameras flashed, and Governor King made a dedicatory speech naming the airport Barnstable Municipal Airport, Boardman-Polando Field, a name which appears on all aviation charts the world over. It is a great honor and deeply appreciated by us all.

By the time we assembled for the banquet, we should have been dead tired for it had been a long, arduous and emotional day, but we were too excited to be tired. In addition to all my other friends, one very special man was present, Bob Stevens, our backer and friend from 1931 and he had brought the little American flag that we had carried on the flight and had graced his office, along with several pictures of us, in the Pentagon.

The banquet was a huge success. There were 1,063 people there to enjoy the festivities. Friends came from everywhere. A group of Daedalians came from Portsmouth, New Hampshire as did Dick Jackson, a good friend from Rochester, New Hampshire. Clark McCurdy presented me with a beautiful replica of the CAPE COD and Dode was given a scrimshaw locket by Sam Sirkis commemorating the flight, as was Jane Boardman Teglas, Russell Boardman's daughter, who shared the honors with us. As I looked over the sea of familiar faces, all I could think of was how can anyone have a thousand friends. I know I am a very lucky man

It would have been really complete if I could have shared it with Russell. I am deeply grateful to all those who gave of their time and effort to make this such a special occasion, and especially Arnie for making the flight from Floyd Bennett field possible, and to Sam Sirkis for masterminding the whole glorious affair.

21

50th Anniversary Celebrations

•

There are just a few of us left who remember with a chuckle, a grin, and a sigh, and sometimes a tear, the good old days. Many of those we remember are no longer with us. Gone are the Avros, the Bristol Bullet, the Jennys, the J-6 Standard, except, perhaps in museums with a "Do Not Touch" sign on them. Gone are many of the great ones—Duke Crance, who flew for the *Daily News*; gone is Peter Brooks, owner and editor of *Liberty Magazine*; gone too are Casey Jones, Burt Acosta, Jimmy Taylor, and Jimmy Haizlip. Who remembers Dick Merritt, who flew the Atlantic both ways? How about Earl Banks in his 504K AVRO or George Watkins? How about Eddie Dunn, who lost his wings on an outside loop? Do you recall "Burr" Laison, who flew the Bristol Bullett skywriting and misspelled *Boston Advertiser?* Not many of us are left who remember Colonel Green and his field in South Dartmouth, Massachusetts.

Roger Q. Williams is still around. I get a poem from him from time to time. Some of you may remember even farther back to 1925-26 when the Guard was at Mitchell Field for summer camp. I grin every time I think of the C6 Standard with the sign "Iron Horse" cruising over Manhattan three nights a week. The pilot had an inner tube just in case he ended up in the Hudson River or Long Island Sound or the East River.

It was a great age we were born into and I think we served it well. All I can say is, we were really lucky and we all loved it more than anything.

Aero Club of New England presented the Jeffrey L. Cabot Award to John Polando on the fiftieth anniversary of the record-breaking flight of Russell N. Boardman and John L. Polando from Floyd Bennett Field, New York, to Instanbul, Turkey, on July 28–30, 1931. Pictured are Larry Glick, John L. Polando, and Dean Edmunds.

Flight in Mr. Sprague's 1931 Stinson from Floyd Bennett Field, New York, to Hyannis, Massachusetts, July 25, 1981.

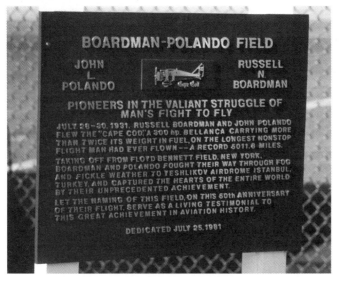

John Polando and plaque at the Barnstable Municipal Airport, Boardman-Polando Field.

Eugene Cernan, principal speaker at the Banquet with John.

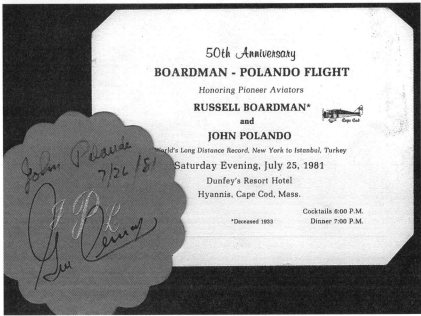

John Polando at the banquet (top) and the invitation.

22

Reminiscences

•

by Dode Polando

Although it began in an ordinary way, July 18, 1985, was a fateful day. I had returned to work part-time in a firm that had been a haven for me from 1972 until I retired in 1981. The people were old friends and the work was rewarding for I take delight in working with people and dealing with figures in my account books. After a most unsatisfactory retirement to part-time employment as a telephone operator and another stint as an office clerk, I was more than happy to be back at the "old stand."

The morning of July 18, John had finally, after many delays due to bad weather, planned a trip to Connecticut to pick up a propeller that had been repaired for a friend. He was chipper, rising early on that bright, sunny day with a grin and a spring in his step that had been absent for several weeks. He had invited an old friend to accompany him just for the fun of it. As I recall, he left the house before I did because he had to have the plane back at Hyannis Aviation for it was booked for a job at one o'clock.

As I drove contentedly to work along the Mid-Cape highway, I was congratulating John and myself on our continued good fortune. John was doing what he did best and loving it—flying. I was going to a job I thoroughly enjoyed with people I liked and, since this was Thursday, pay day, I was looking forward to a challenging morning with my account books.

All went well until about 11:30 a.m. when the telephone rang. The call was from the airport. The familiar voice on the other end of the line was apologetic and hesitant. "I have something to tell you," Bruce said, "but I hardly know how to say it. John has been in an accident. He seems to be okay except that he struck his head and had to have some stitches. Joe Boylen, his passenger and friend, is all right but he hurt his back. I really don't know a lot more than

Johnnie Polando 1981

that. They crashed on takeoff and it looks like the plane is a total. But don't panic. I'll go down and pick them up this afternoon."

I was conditioned to the problems inherent in aviation careers. I had panicked long ago when John and I first met and a B-17 had crashed in Utah and all aboard were lost. I had dashed off a hasty letter to John and in return received a telephone call at two in the morning from John. John was comforting but firm. "I'm fine, but, if this is the way you are going to react every time there's a crash, I won't be seeing you anymore. Flying is my life. It's no more dangerous than a lot of other professions, but it has made a fatalist out of me and every pilot I know. When your time comes, there will be little or nothing you can do about it. I do everything I can to avoid trouble but things happen that you can't prevent and you just have to live with the risks or die a thousand times over from fear." It was clear that I had to live by his rules or find another friend.

Thereafter I managed to cope and finally became comfortable with the possibility that one day I might get a call. Actually, I knew John so well that I didn't have a problem with it. John had a great deal of pride in his unblemished record and would do absolutely nothing to tarnish his image. He was extremely thorough in his preflight routine and adhered closely to his check list. He made me feel that he was invincible and, if something unforeseen occurred, he would be able to deal with it.

This feeling of confidence kept me from saying anything about Bruce's call at the office. It also made it possible for me to go home without stopping at the airport. Bruce had said that it would be best if I didn't turn up looking anxious. I must admit the wait for the telephone call from Bruce was very difficult. I cooked and baked and did all sorts of small jobs just to keep busy, but, it didn't keep my mind off the accident and John's condition.

Finally I got a call from Bruce, who was still at the Rockville General Hospital. He said he was sorry to call again but, "I thought it best that you know that John looks terrible. His eyes are black, his nose is bandaged because of the stitches, and he had lost a lot of blood but, in spite of that, he insists on coming home. Joe is being kept overnight because he hurt his back and more x-rays are needed before releasing him." The telephone clicked and Bruce was gone.

It was a couple of hours before the headlights of Bruce's car brought me to the kitchen door. John looked worse than Bruce had described. He was ashen from the loss of blood. Bruce and I each took an arm and literally carried John into the house. The eyes were the blackest I have ever seen. His nose was bandaged so that it looked like it had been broken though I was sure that it had not. There was no jaunty grin, no bounce to his faltering steps as there had been that morning. John was trying valiantly to hold back the tears. The hurt was so deep and the agony so obvious that I was at a loss as to how to help. John's greatest concern was Joe's injuries. He was full of apologies for the accident, for it had been caused by an unforgivable oversight—one John could not believe he had made and one for which he would never forgive himself.

As John was taking off for Hyannis, after having lunch with friends, and picking up the repaired propeller, he and Joe did the ground check then boarded the plane in preparation for departure. John filed for departure, fastened his seat belt but did not buckle the shoulder harness because he was too short to reach the radio with it secured. Joe was struggling with his seat belt and harness and had moved his seat back as far as the track would permit. Only then did John realize that he had failed to remove the gustlock, which now was locked in place in the post and wouldn't budge. Takeoff was impossible at this point so John swerved the plane to the right in an effort to protect Joe on impact with the pile of dirt. This probably saved their lives but the plane was a total. The force of the blow wrenched Joe's back severely and John struck his head on the instrument panel knocking himself out briefly. After getting no response from John, Joe got out of the plane and started back to the hangar for help. John came to and unfastened his belt then, bleeding profusely, attempted to get out of the plane. One of the workmen came running over and helped him but insisted that he lie down because he was bleeding badly and await the arrival of the ambulance.

The emergency team did a wonderful job of stanching the blood that poured from the gash in John's nose and eyebrows. They took both John and Joe immediately to the Rockville hospital. John's face required twenty-four stitches to close the wound. The blow had ruptured the blood vessels, and great pockets of blood appeared under the blackened eyes.

Even at this point John's greatest concern was Joe and the plane, not himself. After taking extensive head x-rays, at the hospital they reluctantly permitted John to fly home with Bruce. No one

John and Dorothy (Dode) Polando.

could have been more concerned, more comforting and helpful than Bruce. He did not criticize the unfortunate affair, only gave moral as well as physical support in John's time of trouble.

The following day, Friday, July 19, I took John to the emergency room at the Cape Cod Hospital, where his own doctor, Roger Chabra, removed the bandages, cleaned the wound, and rebandaged his face. He then took some blood. Dr. Chabra suggested that John might need a transfusion and that he would call us Monday morning if that was the case. He remarked that John was a very lucky man for he seemed to be recovering well.

I have never seen John so upset, so depressed, so demoralized. He wept off and on all of Friday, Saturday, and Sunday. He was on the telephone to the Rockville hospital to check on Joe. He called and apologized to Penny, Joe's wife. He made almost as many outgoing calls as he had incoming to inquire for Joe's well-being. The nights were the worst. He slept fitfully. He couldn't understand how he had made such a stupid mistake. His concern for Joe was constant. The pressure he put on himself for having made an error was continuous. He refused to be comforted by anyone. He struggled through the three days with some improvement in his black eyes. The stitches were healing nicely, but his mood was blacker than the eyes and more painful than the stitches. Yet, aside from the extreme depression, he seemed to be in remarkably good shape. He was not even sore from the accident, which is incredible.

Dr. Chabra called Monday morning saying that John needed to have a blood test that day then go into the outpatient for two units of blood on Tuesday. There seemed to be no other injuries. Monday afternoon we went to the hospital for the blood test and walked the equivalent of a short city block to the laboratory. John was slow but refused to be helped as we went down the corridor. His foul mood and feisty nature were evident when a man squeezed into line in front of me. I had insisted that John sit down and I would give the receptionist the necessary information. John got very incensed and said "Hey, what do you think you are doing, pushing in front of my wife?" The man mumbled something about being there before us, and John said that if he felt better he would have punched him in the nose.

John was due at the hospital for the transfusion at 7:30 A.M. on Tuesday. He was up early and started to shave while I prepared breakfast. He had just about finished when he called to me, saying that his knees were weak. I found him holding onto the doorjamb. With his arm around my shoulders, we made it to the chair in the den, where he had coffee. I helped him dress because he wasn't able to get out of the chair. He complained of having a headache, something he had never had in the forty-one years we had been married. I gave him two Bufferin. By now the time was getting short, so I helped him into a small rocking chair and dragged him across the den, down the hall, and through the living room and the kitchen to the back door. Both he and I attributed his weakness to the loss of blood and the headache, too. With great effort he managed to get to the car using a chairback as a crutch, then dropped limply into the front seat. We left immediately for the hospital.

All the way he complained of a terrible headache. I was so alarmed that I went to the emergency entrance and ran in for help to get John out of the car and on to a gurney. It was 7:20 A.M. By this time John had a strange pallor and an attempt to take a blood sample produced nothing. I was frantic, for the medics were not

Johnnie Polando 1981

moving fast enough to suit me. They dared not give him anything until they could determine his condition.

It was just after eight o'clock when his doctor came to the waiting room where I had been sent while they worked on John. He was sure that John had had a massive brain hemorrhage and would have to have immediate surgery and said that the chances of his surviving were slim.

The operation started before ten o'clock, and it was almost one before he was taken to the recovery room. He was alive, but barely. I had called all the children to give them as much information on their father as possible. John lay in intensive care for five days, hovering between life and death. He could not respond to anything or anybody. His heart was strong and his body was able but the damage to the brain stem was irreversible. He died quietly twenty-one days after the surgery, August 11, 1985.

John would not like to be remembered for the way he died but for the way he lived. His greatest love was flying, and he gave his very best to it and to his family and friends. His accomplishment were many, his failures few. I feel that his spirit lives on in the hearts of those who knew and loved him best.

All of the foregoing was written by me, Dode Polando, with John's often reluctant assistance, for he was at heart a modest man. Because his love of flying and sharing experiences with his host of friends was verbal, the events were his but the words are mine.

My life began when we met. Our life together produced three wonderful, caring children and an endless store of fond and funny memories as well as some sobering events.

To say that I was not a part of John's life in the 1930s when much of these events took place does not mean that I have not reaped great joy from his recounting them to me. I am extremely proud of his many accomplishments, his successes and failures, for who of us has not benefited from both the highs and lows of life. I know I have.